MY CUBA LIBRE

My older Sister, Great Grandmother, Grandmother and Mother in Villa Viejo

MY CUBA LIBRE

Bringing Fidel Castro to Justice

George J. Fowler, III

STORY MERCHANT BOOKS
BEVERLY HILLS
2013

ISBN 10: 0989715426
ISBN 13: 9780989715423

Story Merchant Books
9601 Wilshire Boulevard #1202
Beverly Hills CA 90210
http://www.storymerchant.com/books.html

Cover and interior design by Robert Aulicino.
Cover photos: Castro: Getty Images, scale: istockphoto.com

PREFACE

FIDEL IS STILL ALIVE.

The Cuban sun on my face would wake me. I would open my eyes, hear the birds, and smell the sweet fragrance of the *mariposas*.[1] I'd jump out of bed and dress up like Roy Rogers, who I thought was a Cuban. I also thought Mickey Mantle and Roger Maris of the New York Yankees were Cuban. They all spoke Spanish on Cuban TV. My Cuba was paradise. But one morning, sometime before dawn, I was awakened by the sound of gunshots. As my mother had taught me, I dropped to the floor. Our lives were about to change dramatically. It was January 1, 1959, and I was only nine years old.

Later in the day, I heard chanting and shouting—but there was no cheering coming from my home. "Fowler" might not seem like a Cuban name, but our roots in Cuba go back to the nineteenth century; we are as Cuban as they come. My parents owned a modest, fairly modern house right on the edge of El Laguito, Havana, in the Country Club neighborhood. We lived in the shadow of my great-grandfather's home, Villa Viejo: a five-story mansion with gardeners and a staff of seventeen. That day, there was no cheering coming from Villa Viejo either.

Fidel Castro slowly worked his way toward Havana, making

---

[1] Cuba's national flower, a white ginger. In Spanish *mariposa* means butterfly.

sure he had total control of the city before he moved in ten days later. His control soon extended over the whole island. Since then, he has worked to maintain his power above all else. Castro betrayed Cuba: destroying a nation, dividing a people, and causing untold suffering. My family was just one of thousands that the dictator uprooted and plundered.

This book is about the horrors of Castro's Cuba and how his five decade old dictatorship savaged thousands of families, including my own.

Our lives in danger, we fled to the United States and settled in Fort Lauderdale, Florida. All of my family's assets were wiped out; two years later, my father chose to end his life. My mother moved us to San Juan, Puerto Rico, where I worked hard as a construction laborer. I moved to New Orleans to attend college, and the United States became my adopted homeland once more. Like many Cuban exiles, I survived and eventually thrived in America. Intelligent, enterprising, and capitalists at heart, Cubans are one of the most successful immigrant groups in the United States. If you want to see what the Cubans can do in a free economy, visit Miami.

Cuban Americans like me are proud defenders of this, the greatest nation on earth. I thank God for this country and its generous people and delight that my children and grandchildren have the privilege to call themselves Americans.

While Cuban exiles came to prosper in America, those who stayed behind faced poverty, despair, and a brutal authoritarian regime. Castro filled his prisons with anyone who dared to oppose or question him, and countless brave Cubans were unjustly tortured or killed. Government neglect and mismanagement led to widespread hunger and disease, and those who tried to escape were murdered or jailed. The U.S. made only one half-hearted attempt to dethrone Castro: the disastrous Bay of Pigs invasion in 1961. President Kennedy abandoned the courageous Cuban volunteer fighters of Brigade 2506 and left them to face Castro's army alone. Since then, the international community has made no serious attempt to free Cuba, and the people continue to suffer.

After I graduated from LSU, I studied at Tulane Law School and entered the field of maritime law and worked under some of the best lawyers in the world. Eventually, I became successful enough to start my own firm. But as much as I grew to love America, I could never forget my homeland. I heard many horrible stories of the regime's cruelty, excess, and neglect. Like many other exiles, I dreamed of ways to remove Castro from power and bring freedom to my people. But rather than resort to violence, I struggled through legal means to bring him to account for his crimes. I am a lawyer to the bone and trust in the rule of law.

In the early 1990s, I had the good fortune of meeting a truly remarkable man: Jorge Mas Canosa, the founder of the Cuban American National Foundation ("the Foundation"). The Foundation's mission is to bring democracy to Cuba through nonviolent means while advocating for Cuban exiles in the U.S. and abroad. Mas Canosa asked if I could provide the Foundation with legal advice, and soon I agreed to serve pro bono as General Counsel. Since then, I have made numerous legal efforts on the behalf of the Cuban people, many of which I will describe in this book. We battled to keep Elián González in the United States; lobbied for Cuban interests in Washington, D.C.; and fought legal skirmishes with slanderers and publications like *The New York Times*.

Most importantly, we worked incessantly to bring Fidel Castro to trial for his crimes against humanity. I will describe many of his crimes in this book. While Fidel has evaded indictment so far, we will not stop until he faces justice. We prepared a massive criminal complaint—in Spain it's called a *Querella*—for the *Audiencia Nacional*, the notorious Spanish international court. We gathered testimony and affidavits from hundreds of Cubans whose family members were tortured or killed by Castro—terrible stories that needed to be told. We also battled to have Castro indicted in the United States after his fighter planes shot down two defenseless aircraft, killing all aboard, in the Brothers to the Rescue shoot-down. The lawsuits brought much-needed attention to our cause—and kept Castro on his toes. But that's all it did. Castro has not been brought to justice. He must be indicted.

Whenever our efforts seemed to garner interest, Castro's agents would send me little messages to let me know that they were paying attention. I'd get anonymous threatening phone calls or mysterious postcards in the mail. One postcard had a New Orleans stamp to let me know that they were watching me in my own city. The postcard said, *"Jorgito, why don't you come visit us in Cuba?"* It was signed, "Fidel." I gave it to the FBI.

In 1999, I went before the U.S. Congress to present a case for Castro's criminal indictment for murder. Two weeks later, I learned that Castro had talked about me in a public speech and had ranted on for hours. I was glad to hear that he had mentioned me; it meant that our efforts had gotten to him. A defector from his security team once told me that Castro was deeply afraid of being indicted and extradited like Chile's General Pinochet. Castro had given the defector instructions to prevent his arrest by any means, including preventative murder.

In that speech, Castro attacked the Cuban American National Foundation leadership, including Jorge Mas Canosa and his son, Jorge Mas Santos. Castro went on to condemn Roberto Martin Perez, a former Foundation Director who was imprisoned and tortured in Cuba for twenty-seven years. Castro also defamed Francisco "Pepe" José Hernández, co-founder and president of the Foundation. Pepe is a staunch ally, and I'm proud of all the work we do together against the dictator. The

Foundation has associated me with true Cuban patriots and—
after thirty years of working together—good friends.

There are many others whose hard work, courage, and sac-
rifice must be acknowledged.

This book is dedicated to all those who were killed, imprisoned, tortured or displaced by Fidel Castro, many of whom I
write about in this book. In particular, I want to remember my
uncle "Tío" Alberto Fowler who taught me to love that beautiful piece of land in the Caribbean where I was born. He so loved
Cuba that he first fought with Castro expecting that he was
going to oust the dictator, Fulgencio Batista, and replace him
with a democratically elected government. When he realized
that Castro had betrayed Cuba, he joined the valiant Bay of Pig
invaders, who fought until they ran out of ammunition, was captured, imprisoned and tortured. *U.S. News and World Report*
reported that Alberto and 37 of the invaders held off thousands
of Castro's men defending a strategically located rotunda
through the night of April 18, 1961.

I also want to acknowledge my mother-in-law, Mercedes
Jenkins, who with her husband imprisoned, was forced to send
her four little girls away from their beautiful home in Varadero
Beach to prevent them from being sent to communist Russia.
With unflinching dignity, she endured countless humiliations in
order to help her imprisoned husband.

I bend my knee to the courageous American Commander,
William Morgan, who when facing Castro's firing squad refused
to bend a knee and when one knee was shot, refused to bend the
other one and then they shot that knee. Then the rats slaughtered him.

I salute Oswaldo Payá, Cuba's foremost dissident murdered
but a few months ago by Fidel Castro's goons. He was a personal hero to many of us. We will not forget his courage or his
murder.

I also want to acknowledge and thank those who continue to

struggle against Castro in Cuba. They are an example of pure courage. In particular, I recognize the Ladies in White, who armed only with white flowers and their faith in God, protest Castro's inhumanities and are regularly attacked and beaten. I salute Yoani Sanchez, the brave young blogger who has been repeatedly beaten by Castro's thugs because she refuses to end her blogs that denounce Castro's inhumanity. I have high hopes for the dissident, Guillermo "El Coco" Fariñas, who leads the largest dissident group in Cuba and has endured twenty-four hunger strikes against Castro.

I have had the privilege of working with many men and women who over five decades of Castro's dictatorship refuse to give up. In particular, I thank the Directors, Trustees and staff of the Foundation and its human rights organization, the Foundation for Human Rights, especially my personal friends, Clara Maria and Mario del Valle, Juan Gutierrez, Miguel Angel Martinez, Pepe Hernandez, Jorge Mas Santos, Irma Mas Canosa, Tony Costa, Carlos Quintela, Jerónimo Estevez, Laly Sampedro, Omar Lopez Montenegro, and Carlos Garcia.

Many other Cuban exile organizations struggle for our same cause. I single out my friend Jose Basulto, President of the Brothers to the Rescue, and the Bay of Pigs invasion force, La Brigada 2506.

I know I don't have to thank my wife because our hearts are one on this subject. She is my Cuban steel magnolia, unbending and intolerant of abuses and generous of heart. My two children, George and Cristi have always shared my dream. Once when things were getting difficult, I felt that I didn't have the right to put them in danger and so I asked them if they wanted me to stop my work. They were offended by my question.

Over the years, the Cuban refugees here in New Orleans have helped Cuban rafters and refugees, as well as staged many demonstrations. My extended family here in New Orleans has always been there to provide help and support to our noble cause. I was asked to assist a thirteen year old girl named Laura, who much like Elián González, barely made it alive to New Orleans on a sinking boat. She saw her father drown and, thereafter, dehydrated, went into a coma. The doctors and nurses at Ochsner Hospital in New Orleans, who provided wonderful free care, didn't have hope for her recovery. I brought over a little plastic image of La Virgen de la Caridad de Cobre, Cuba's Virgin Mary, and we prayed for her to get well; which miraculously she did. My first cousin, Maria Crumley, who calls herself the Cuban Flan Queen, took Laura into her home as one of her children and nursed her until Laura fully recuperated. One of thousands of stories of compassion and love.

This is my story, but it is also the story of Cubans' thirst for justice. It is a story of unfinished business. I write because Castro is still free. Thousands are murdered and tortured, the Cuban people suffer on a massive scale—and yet Castro walks the earth as a free man. This is more than one country's tragedy; it is an international disgrace. I write to raise awareness of our struggle, to convince the world to *take action*. Fidel Castro cannot be allowed to spend his final years in luxury and power. Whoever becomes his successor after his death will only continue his legacy of bloodshed, cruelty, and hate. We must act *now* to bring freedom to the people of Cuba.

Castro likes to imply that the Cuban exiles who work against him only want their "properties" back. That is not so with me; I am much greedier. I want *all* of Cuba back—free and without Castro.

LOS FOWLERS

THE VERY FIRST AMERICAN FOWLERS WERE ENGLISHMEN WHO traveled to New York in the 1600s. The family remained loyal to the king during the American Revolution. Once the war ended, they moved to Canada after the English Crown gave them deeded lands in Nova Scotia. The Fowlers were soon dispatched as diplomats to Cuba, where they settled down and eventually got into the sugar business.

The Fowlers remained citizens of England and resided in Havana. In 1852, they owned a sugar mill, called La Narcisa, in an area called Yaguajay, close to the small port of Caibarién in Las Villas Province. In that era, Generalissimo Máximo Gómez, the military leader of Cuba's revolution against the Spaniards, established his war camp at La Narcisa. The historian Marcos Iglesias noted that the Generalissimo wrote many of his letters from there. Cuba's foremost historian, Orestes Ferrara, wrote this about Gómez:

> The General slept tranquil for the first time in three years and under a roof. He was in the Narcisa Sugar Mill, owned by the Fowler brothers, descendants of an English father, who were very Cubanized and who had contributed generously to the cause of the independence.[2]

---

[2] Orestes Ferrara, *Memorias* (Antonio Montoto, 1975), p. 125.

Our family has a long tradition of supporting Cuban freedom. Writing about the province of Las Villas, Ferrara wrote:

> In both parts of the province, the Fowler brothers, Cubans and patriots, although children of an Englishman who had been Consul of his country for many years, extended their lands throughout many areas, desiring to give to the fertile tropic [land] Nordic energy.[3]

For nearly 200 years, Cubans—both at home and abroad—have shown their courage fighting for freedom in their country. Cubans had been bravely fighting the Spaniards for decades before Teddy Roosevelt and his Rough Riders came on the scene in 1898. The Cubans were famous for fiercely attacking the Spanish ranks with just their machetes, and *La Carga de el Machete*—the "Charge of the Machete"—struck terror in the hearts of the well-trained Spanish infantry. Many of the chargers would fall to musket fire, but those who broke through the front lines wreaked havoc. When I was little, the Cuban history books attributed the victory over the Spaniards to *La Carga de el Machete*, not to the Rough Riders. I presume the truth lies somewhere in the middle.

Cuba's war of independence was split into three wars. One was the ten year war (1868-1878), the little war (1879-1880), and finally the decisive war of independence (1895-1898). That war against Spain became the Spanish American War. This final war began on February 24, 1895, and was waged throughout the island. The leader of the independence movement against Spain was Cuba's foremost patriot, José Martí. Martí was fearful that the United States would ultimately annex Cuba before the revolution could free the island from Spain.

Another leader of the revolution was Major General Antonio

---

[3] Orestes Ferrara, *Memorias* (Antonio Montoto, 1975), p. 125.

Maceo. Like Martí, Máximo Gómez and Maceo, the rebels were known as Mambises, after the black Spanish officer, Juan Ethnnius Mamby who joined the fight for independence. Today when we want to honor an anti-Castro Cuban, we call him a Mambí. During the height of the revolution, at the end of 1897 there were 240,000 Spanish regulars and 60,000 irregulars on the island. The Cuban revolutionaries were far outnumbered, but they fought bravely and tenaciously. It was a bloody, vicious war. The Spanish General Valeriano Weyler Nicolau used terror methods to subdue the brave rebels. One of those methods was to order all countryside residents to gather in certain areas in towns occupied by his troops. It is estimated that during this war one-third of Cuba's population died through disease and inhumane conditions.

José Martí was killed in his own *Carga de el Machete* on May 19, 1895 as he rode his beautiful white horse at a place called Dos Ríos. Better with words than he was with the machete, Martí wrote this memorable line:

I am good, and like a good man, I shall die with my face to the sun.

And so he did, as did so many others. Facing Castro's firing squads at el paredón (the wall), thousands died screaming, "Viva Cristo Rey"—"Long live Christ the King!" But that came later.

After Martí's death, Máximo Gómez and Antonio Maceo continued the fight. Maceo died on December 7, 1896 in Havana province while returning from the west. That left Máximo Gómez as the foremost leader of the revolution. The rebel forces defeated the Spanish in various battles and the Spaniards were kept on the defensive. Much like our own war of independence, the Cubans were winning the war simply by maintaining a military presence on the island.

Americans sympathized with the Cuban rebels and our

newspapers called for U.S. intervention. The battleship USS MAINE was sent to Havana in the last week of January and on February 15, 1898, the USS MAINE suffered a major explosion that killed 258 of the crew sinking the ship. In the United States, Spain was quickly blamed for the explosion. In my history books in Cuba, the question was not so clear. It was rumored that the rebel forces blew up the USS MAINE in order to force the Americans to come to their aid.

On April 11, 1898, President McKinley asked Congress to allow him to send American troops to Cuba to end the war there. On April 19, Congress passed resolutions supporting Cuban independence and disclaiming any intention to annex Cuba. The Americans entered the war and on July 17, 1898, Spain conceded and ultimately signed a protocol of peace with the United States agreeing to free Cuba. The Fowlers were elated. They were English Mambises.

In 1895, in the last years of the war of independence, Winston Churchill (one of my heroes) came to Cuba at the invitation of the Spanish government. At the time, Churchill opposed the Cuban revolution and was sympathetic to the Spanish Crown. He was a royalist. He came to our sugar mill, Narcisa, to present his credentials to my great, great-grandfather the English Consul. I suspect the two of them had their disagreements. But years later, Winston Churchill admitted in a letter to his mother that he was wrong for opposing Cuban independence.

My great-grandfather, George R. Fowler, owned four sugar mills—Dos Hermanas, Concepcion, Parque Alto, and La Narcisa—and the Moron Railroad of Cuba. George lost three of the mills in the 30s during the reign of Presidente Gerardo Machado, one of Cuba's dictators. I do not know whether his dictatorship had any connection to the loss of the three mills or whether it was due to the depression. However, La Narcisa was by far the largest and most profitable and we still owned it when I was born in 1950.

After Cuba was free from the Spaniards, the Fowlers went to work in their businesses. By the 1890s, Narcisa had become a substantial sugar mill with many miles of rail and electricity. It moved its sugar by rail to the Port of Caibarién en route to international ports. The mill was nicknamed "The Colossus of Las Villas" during the good times and *"Las Vacas Gordas"* ("The Fat Cows") when sugar prices were high.

When I was born, Narcisa employed over five thousand people in lands that extended over forty-five miles. Its lands were magnificent; rolling hills dotted with the tall, stately, white Cuban royal palms.

In the 1930s, 40s, and 50s, Narcisa was administered by a Greek named Constantino Bourbakis Aristopavlos. Bourbakis was known as the best sugar man in Cuba. Quiet and solitary, he lived in the top floor of *La Casa de Vivienda*, the Fowler residence at Narcisa. He knew techniques for producing the largest sugar crystals. In 1958, just before Castro seized power, the mill produced over 330,000 sacks of sugar that weighed 250 pounds each. It also produced over 1,770,000 gallons of honey. Today it produces nothing.

My grandfather, George, ran the mill but lived mostly on his yacht—the *Narcisa II*. He anchored the yacht in the city of Nassau in the Bahamas. He and Bourbakis frequently wrote to each other long letters about the business affairs of the mill.

My grandmother, Lise Perrilliat—or "Mama Lise," as we called her—was the only child of a well-known Louisiana French family. Pretty and petite, she was descended from the first Creole settlers of New Orleans. She traveled extensively with her father, who brought along a tutor and a piano. He gave her a classical education in Greek and Latin, and she had a lifelong love of literature and writing. With her father and mother, she made the historic first crossing of the Panama Canal, along with numerous transatlantic crossings. She was even booked on the Titanic for the fateful voyage but fortunately changed her plans because she got the measles.

Lise's French-born father, General Arsène Perrilliat, was an engineer and professor at Tulane University. An officer with the Corps of Engineers, he traveled to the Suez Canal to study the water flow and helped design New Orleans's levees (the ones that held in Katrina). He was friends with Thomas Edison.

Both the Perrilliats and the Fowlers vacationed in Long Island, where Lise and George met as teenagers. There they fell in love. The Perrilliats were concerned because George was too young and too rich. But Mama Lise was head over heels. After making her New Orleans debut (like my daughter, Cristi, did), Lise married my grandfather and moved to Narcisa, where she built housing for the workers, a school, and a church. She was greatly loved by the people of Narcisa. They had five children and raised them between Narcisa and Havana. The eldest, George Jr., was my father.

Lise loved Narcisa, which gave her the peace to write her poetry and books. A quiet, scholarly person, she wrote a beautiful book of poems called *Listen My Children*. She also wrote about Narcisa in her book La Zafra (The Harvest). In one passage, she describes life at the mill:

> Our eight-year-old Fiat wheezed and sneezed its way along the narrow gauge railroad track on its way to Narcisa. We were going down to the sugar mill for the opening of the "*Zafra*," or grinding season.
>
> *Zafra* is a word used a hundred times a day in the language of the planter; it means "crop," but particularly the sugar crop. It may also refer to the duration of the crop— one speaks of a good or bad *Zafra*, a long or short *Zafra*.

It's a tricky word, but after mastering it, one soon learns to use its multiple meanings.

It was early February. We expected to start grinding within the next few days if the weather held out. We wanted to arrive in time to hear the first low rumble of the mill, as the big engines turned the immense wheels of the machinery that started off the *Zafra*. There was something imposing in that sound.

The mill reminded one of a great monster that had been quiet for six months or more, and—all of sudden—had awakened hungry and growling for food. We wanted to see him have his first meal, and also to see the heavy-laden little cane ears come rolling in like fat green caterpillars to be gobbled up by the giant beast.

The children couldn't wait to hear the sound of the big mill whistle blow for the first time, as it announced the opening of the season. There was always speculation as to who would blow it. Each year, my husband would take one of the children high up a narrow ladder, which led to the boiler-house, and allow him to turn on the steam. It was fun to hear the first deep moan, which grew louder and louder until the vibrations were deafening. Narcisa's whistle, I'm quite sure, rivaled the "Queen Mary's." People swore it could be heard three miles distant. My first year, as a bride, I had blown it, and our manager said that I had brought good luck, as we had ground a very large *Zafra*. The following years, as the children grew up, they each had a turn.

For miles around the workers would wait anxiously for the sound of the whistle to announce the happy event to the entire countryside. This sound meant for them to go back to work, hard work but happy work because it brought prosperity. It meant money, and all the good things that money could buy.

No wonder the first day of *Zafra* everybody was in a holiday mood as they greeted everyone else. They laughed and joked, made bets on the outcome of the *Zafra*: "How many tons will be ground? How long will it last? June, perhaps July?" All in all, this was a great day, a "*día de fiesta*."

I loved Narcisa and as a little boy rode horseback (with my Roy Rogers outfit) through its beautiful hills. I remember well the sounds and smells of the sugar mill and its trains during the grinding season. Some may describe the pungent molasses aroma as a bad smell. It smelled like heaven to me. I still can smell it if I force myself to remember. I visit the Fanjul[4] family's sugar mill in La Romana, Santo Domingo, just to catch that smell.

My grandfather was an elegant, handsome gentleman who lived a lavish, fast life. He had white hair that contrasted with his perennial tan. Mother said the women in Havana's society threw themselves at him. His best friend in Cuba was Julio Lobo, a trader and financier known as the "Sugar King"; the two owned a bank together. George worked hard to develop Narcisa into the successful mill it was. He added a rice mill, 10,000 head of cattle, and a railroad.

During the Second World War, George built a distillery with the capacity to produce up to 20,000 liters of alcohol a day. Our "Don Alberto" brandy and "Fowler" rum were bottled by the Bacardis. My good friend Clara del Valle, a political ally and one of the owners of Bacardi Rum, jokingly claims Fowler rum tasted like piss. I disagree. I have one bottle left and will drink it when Fidel Castro is gone. It will taste like the best rum in the world.

---

[4]The Fanjuls are a sugar family from Cuba who have impressive sugar holdings in Santo Domingo, Florida and Louisiana. They are known as the Sugar Barons. They are friends.

While Lise adored Narcisa, she did not enjoy Havana's extravagant, wild life. Her marriage to George ended in what may have been one of Cuba's first divorces, which became a public scandal.

In Cuba's Spanish-influenced culture, women could go to the many elaborate parties at Havana and Varadero Beach, but they were expected to obey their husbands and act conservative in every manner. Women had to stay virginal before marriage and faithful to their generally unfaithful husbands—no matter what. If you think that this formula makes for lousy marriages, you are right. My grandaunt told me that in Cuba if you were a poor woman accused of adultery, they called you a whore. If you were rich, you were called a "crazy girl."

Divorce in those days was totally unacceptable and nearly unknown in Cuba. Havana's society treated women badly if they were not "tolerant," so most Cuban women accepted their husbands' philandering ways. Mama Lise did not. She moved to New Orleans to soothe her grief over her failed marriage. She continued to love George passionately until she died, and her sadness is reflected in her poems.

MOTHER

My mother, Graciela Estevez, was the only grandchild of Julian Aguilera, a conservative businessman of Spanish descent. She respected her grandfather greatly and told me that though he may not have been the wealthiest man in Cuba, he certainly paid the most taxes. A man of integrity, Julian built a fortune in Cuban real estate holdings—some of the properties are still registered in his name. He only built a new property after he had paid for the last one.

Mother was raised in "Villa Viejo," a castle-like home by "El Laguito" in the Country Club section of Havana. Her parents tried to spoil her, but she never spoiled herself. She was frequently absent from school because of kidnapping threats. Kidnapping was big business in Cuba—and still is throughout Latin America.

My great-grandfather Julian supported everybody; no one else on that side of the family worked. My grandfather, Santiago Estevez, was quoted as saying, "Work is so bad they have to pay you to do it." They played golf and partied. My kind, loving godmother, Manina, was Cuba's female golf champion for several years.

I would spot Julian walking Villa Viejo in the early morning hours before he went to work. He wore either a white linen suit or a guayabera (white linen shirt) with a Panama hat. He carried a cane as he checked on his fruit gardens and the farm animals that supplied Villa Viejo's tables. Julian's diligence and work ethic was an inspiration to me, and still is to this day.

Bored with her life in the castle, my mother was excited to meet the Fowlers, who were free to do what they wanted. To my mother they were wild. Mother became fast friends with my father's sister, Lisette, and his dashing brother, Tío Alberto. Mother said that Lisette showed up at the fancy parties in Havana without a stitch of makeup and yet would still be the prettiest girl there. Tío Alberto loved playing pranks on people. One time, they were all invited to attend a rather stiff and formal party. To lighten the mood, Tío Alberto put a couple of little frogs in his mouth; when he went to greet some older ladies, he let the frogs jump out of his mouth.

Through the two of them, Graciela met my father, George, Jr. They were married in an elaborate, highly publicized wedding, and their honeymoon lasted for two months. Mother's life went from dull to outrageously fun. Nothing has ever been like Havana in the pre-Castro days. My parents went out every night to parties and nightclubs. The women were gorgeous, the men elegant in their white linen suits and starched white *Guayaberas*. Some nightclubs, like the Tropicana, had elaborate dance shows.

From the end of the War of Independence (1898) until the early 50's, the Fowlers were uninvolved with politics. We were sugar people and devoted our efforts to the sugar mill and its people. It was a big job and my ancestors, grandfather and father did a credible job. The mill prospered and life in Cuba was wonderful for my family.

Things changed in the early 1950s. Fulgencio Batista y Zaldivar was elected President of Cuba from 1940 to 1944. That first presidency was relatively uneventful. However, he ran for president again in 1952 and, when he lost that election, he led a military coup and took power of the country until Castro ousted him on January 1, 1959. Batista was a greedy, power hungry man. Most Cubans didn't accept this coup and they rebelled.

In 1952, the dictator Batista suspended the 1940 Constitution and eliminated civil liberties. Batista aligned himself with the mafia that controlled Havana's casinos, as well as drugs and prostitution and with American investors.

During the Batista regime, the gap between the rich and the poor widened. But the disgust and distrust of the Batista government was not the problem of only the poor. Cuba's large middle class and upper class were also against Batista and wanted him out. However, with the exception of my uncle, Tío Alberto, who chose to support Castro's rebels against Batista, the Fowlers remained on the sidelines. This was a mistake. We should have been engaged in ensuring that we did not replace one dictator with a much worse dictator. But the truth is that Castro lied to the people of Cuba. He lied about his Christianity and lied about his views on democracy. He was a Marxist; but mostly he was a *Fidelista*. Fidel has always been about Fidel.

I hardly know anyone that speaks well of the dictator Batista. Batista was of mixed races, African, Spanish, Indian and some Chinese. He came from humble origins and joined the military as a young man. Batista led what was called the "Revolt of the Sergeants" and participated in overthrowing the government of Gerardo Machado. Batista always referred to himself as "The Sergeant" because that was his military rank. After Machado, Carlos Manual de Cespedes became president for a short period. Thereafter, Ramon Grau San Martin was made president and Batista became his army chief of staff. He had the rank of colonel which effectively put him in control of the presidency. Ultimately, Batista was elected president in 1940.

Although Batista's dictatorship was distasteful, it was a lot less dangerous than it was corrupt. Batista entered into deals with the mobsters Lucky Luciano, Meyer Lansky, and Santo Trafficante. His relationship with these mobsters and American investors formed the bulk of his earnings. Although there was some corruption between Cuban businessmen and Batista, he really did not have to get in bed with the Cuban businessmen to make a great deal of money.

Although initially the United States government openly supported and protected Batista because of his anti-communist policies, the Cuban people did not want Batista after his coup in 1952. Many formed various anti-Batista rebel groups. One of such groups was led by Fidel Castro Ruz.

On July 26, 1953, a small cadre of revolutionaries led by Fidel Castro attacked the Moncada military barracks in Santiago. The Batista forces easily repelled the attack and jailed its leaders, including Fidel Castro. From then on, Castro's movement was known as the July 26 Movement. The revolution began in earnest against Fulgencio Batista. The people rose up against Batista, who responded with tortures and murders. However, he was unable to capture the rebels in the Sierra Maestra and Escambray Mountains. Secretly, Castro sought out the aid of the Soviet Union who had no love lost for the United States. The Soviet Union began to covertly support Castro and supplied him with weapons. On top of that, in March 1958, the U.S. stopped selling arms to the Cuban government and the U.S. State Department told Batista to leave. Our intelligence in Cuba was not intelligent. The revolution raged on throughout the island and the rebels were winning.

Realizing that the end was near, on December 31, 1958, at a New Years Eve party, Batista announced that he was leaving Cuba and urged his administration to leave also. He flew to the Dominican Republic. At the time, I heard he took $70 million, but others spoke of a personal fortune of more than $300 million. He was welcomed by the vicious dictator of Santo Domingo, Rafael Trujillo, Batista's military ally. Batista eventually found asylum in Europe and died near Marbella, Spain on August 6, 1973. I remember that my stepfather, Emilio Cosculluela, sent the Batista family condolences. I was confused when I heard that. Batista was no good to Cuba and I loved Cuba. However, Emilio's father was the Prime Minister of Public Works under Batista. He was a good and honest man.

The Fowlers had no dealings with Batista. As noted before, during this fifty year period from the war of independence until Castro's coup, the Fowlers were not involved in politics. But the Fowlers and millions of other Cubans were about to experience the most horrendous and cruel dictatorship ever.

Notwithstanding, the lifestyle of 50s in Cuba was spectacular. If you were not involved in politics, life in Cuba was paradise.

HAVANA IN THE 1950s

PEOPLE OFTEN ASKED MY MOTHER IF I WAS ACTUALLY HER child. She and my father both had very fair skin and jet-black hair. I, on the other hand, was so blonde in my early years that my hair looked white. I am a big man with a big head; some people even say I look Russian. A few years ago, while handling a case in Spain, I upset a Spanish prosecutor. When I walked into his office, he jumped in fright, thinking that I was one of the Russian drug dealers he was prosecuting in the *Audiencia Nacional*.

I was born in Havana at the modern Miramar Hospital on Columbus Day, October 12, 1950. I was the middle child and have two siblings—an older sister, Lita, and a younger sister, Lisette. Lita wasn't too happy when I came along; she felt I stole her limelight. I remember playing canasta with her in our beach house when we were young. Extremely intelligent and compassionate, she has worked as a social worker her whole life. My kind and loving little sister, Lisette, is married to the nicest guy in the world, by the name of Luis. The two of them have a great marriage with two boys and one grandchild.

My father, George Jr., looked like the English actor David Niven. He sported a very Cuban thin mustache. Tall, slim, and elegant, he was nicknamed *"El Duque"* (The Duke) because of his impeccable manners. My father was rather absent from my life, preferring to work at the sugar mill, travel, and enjoy the Cuban nightlife. Although I rarely saw him, I remember him taking me out once on his little 15' boat, nicknamed *Mi Yate*— "My Yacht" in English. He called it that to bother his father, who owned a yacht but refused to lend it to him. I remember watching porpoises swimming alongside our boat. It was a beautiful moment.

Sometimes on Saturdays, my father would take me to the Yacht Club in Havana, where I bowled, played baseball, and swam competitively. My father was an excellent swimmer also and had been the captain of the Louisiana State University swim team. He once swam competitively against Johnny Weissmuller, the actor who played Tarzan, although he lost the race. I was taught how to box at the Yacht Club by an old professional boxer, an American who spoke Spanish.

My mother was dazzlingly beautiful and maintained her cocktail-party slim figure through exercise and diet. Elizabeth Taylor was the only woman I thought compared to her in beauty and elegance. Later, when I was a little refugee boy, I even bought her a book about Elizabeth Taylor using the savings from my job selling newspapers.

Every night before she put me to bed, mother would tell me about the places she was going to meet my dad. The names of Havana's famous nightclubs—Tropicana, Montmartre, the Hotel Nacional, Sans Souci—gave me visions of unlimited enjoyment. I never saw them with my own eyes, but the stories she told made them seem like magical places.

When I interviewed her for this book, Mother couldn't stop telling me stories. Her eyes lit up and laughed as she remembered those exciting days. She mingled with everybody, and her only goal was to have fun. She has little regret about her financial losses because she had a ball. Her motto: *Lo bailado nadie te lo quita*—"They can't take away what you have danced."

Vanity Fair's September, 2011 issue had an extensive article on the Tropicana nightclub which mentions my grandfather, George Fowler. Here is a portion:

> In 1956, the Tropicana nightclub premiered its first promotional flight from Miami to Havana on Cubana de Aviacion—it was billed as the "Cabaret in the Sky."
>
> Aileen Mehle, *society columnist*: Tropicana was heaven. You couldn't keep me away. Everything was *yayaya*: smoking and drinking champagne and laughing, having fun. And all those fabulous dances and songs. It was the same every night, the height of glamour, up there with the Ziegfeld *Follies*. It was the only place to go. Cuba was wonderful because it was sexy, especially when you're young and you're a girl and you have friends who will take you to clubs with music all night long. It never stopped. ... I was there every night when I was in Cuba. I used to see all these fellows. There was one they called Beauty, Beauty Cendoya. And Mike Tarafa and Julio Lobo, really great guys, the two richest men in Cuba. And of course I met them all: George Fowler, Pepe Fanjul, and the Sanchezes, Emilio and Marcelo. Everybody was rich then. The fellows that owned the sugar plantations were the only ones I knew. We were young and crazy and drinking, dancing, singing, gambling, and having a wonderful time.

She taught me to enjoy life to the fullest, and even today at 87, I never see her depressed. She continues to take care of her children to this day. She does hate getting old, but doesn't make a big deal out of it—so long as everybody is running around pleasing her. She rejoices in our success and never dwells on our problems or failures. She expected excellence from us, but always with great deal of love. One of my clients, exaggerating but obviously wishing to make a mother proud, told my mother at a firm party in Miami that I was the best maritime lawyer in the world. Her answer: "*Of course, he is my son.*" My victories are her victories. That is okay with me.

In the nightclubs, she hung out with famous entertainers such as Nat King Cole, Frank Sinatra, Rita Hayworth, and Errol Flynn. My mother spent time with Ava Gardner at the Kawama Club in Varadero Beach and remarked upon her large almond eyes. She reluctantly admitted that Ava "may" have been the most beautiful woman in Cuba.

Her self-assurance allowed her to befriend anybody she fancied. She partied with the chorus girls and others who the snobbish society women wouldn't talk to. She even met the mobsters Meyer Lansky and Lucky Luciano.

Mother and father danced into the early morning hours before bringing their friends to the Havana Yacht Club. There they would steal my grandfather's 110' yacht, *Narcisa I*, to continue the fun on the water. The captain of the *Narcisa I* wore a blazer and tie, but refused to wear shoes. Mother said that back then, the Fowlers were known for running into the docks— nothing much has changed!

In the daytime, my parents frequently brought the *Narcisa I* to watch the crew boat races in Varadero Beach. The beach was about a two-hour drive from Havana. Back then the beach was dotted with beautiful homes. It was magical. You could walk for a quarter of a mile into the surf and its crystal waters would barely come up to your hips.

The races culminated in all-night parties, and the winning crews were Cuba's heroes. Different private clubs competed, but the big rivalry was between Havana and Varadero. Varadero's club, founded in 1919, was called *El Club Náutico*. My father-in-law, Eduardo Jenkins, rowed and coached its crew. The club was his pride and joy.

Santiago, my maternal grandfather and a real character, had a home in Varadero by the canal. All the fishing yachts had to go right past this house, and in the early morning they would toot their horn to wake my grandfather. He would get up cussing, and we would laugh. My sisters and I would hunt shrimp in the waters in front of his house. We used lanterns to attract the shrimp and caught them with nets attached to long poles. It was a wonderful time in my childhood.

Havana was a sophisticated, architecturally magnificent city, with historic buildings and homes hundreds of years old. Aside from the nightclub life, the wealthy people in Cuba lived a more formal and aristocratic lifestyle; some families dated back to the conquistadores. In Havana of the 1950s, the social life of the rich centered on its large private clubs: the Havana Yacht Club, the Biltmore, and the Country Club. The last two had golf courses.

Cuba had a large middle class, and they too enjoyed an active social life and had their own clubs. But the classes were separated. Even the dictator Fulgencio Batista, while president, was turned down when he applied for membership in the Havana Yacht Club.

In the 1950s, I spent my time going between four places: my home, Villa Viejo, the LaSalle School, and the Havana Yacht Club. Saturday lunch at Villa Viejo was mandatory. As in most Spanish homes, meals came at precise times. The entire family was supposed to be present, with great-grandfather Julian at the head of the table; however, my father and Santiago's chairs were invariably empty. Now I know they were probably nursing a hangover or catting around, but not a word was ever said about their absence.

This hard-partying lifestyle took its toll on my family. My great-grand-uncle, Don Alberto Fowler, died at the Montmartre

Nightclub after walking into an empty elevator shaft. He was known as *El Principe Indio* (The Indian Prince) because of his dark good looks and eccentric fashion sense—he often wore a turban.

Villa Viejo was like a castle. Ancient Moorish guns, swords, and sables adorned the high ceilings; below them hung ancient tapestries. The house even featured a 300-year-old Moorish cannon that once lay at the bottom of the sea off the Spanish coast.

To a child, the house was kind of creepy. Up the main staircase was a well-oiled full suit of armor with a face painted inside the helmet. At a childhood birthday party, word got around to my friends about the scary armored man. They refused to go upstairs, and the party had to be moved to the garage.

The first floor contained the garages, servants' quarters, and the main kitchen. The second floor had several living rooms, the dining room, another kitchen, and a modern living room with a TV. On the third floor, each of the three couples had two bedrooms and their own living room. Additionally, there was a massage room. The fourth floor was used for sewing; there were always workers up there sewing linens. The basement held my great-grandfather's office and the wine cellar.

Outside was a beautiful farm with orange groves, mango trees of multiple varieties, avocado trees, and Cuba's royal palm trees. We could have fed ourselves with its farm animals—cows, chickens, pigs, ducks, and turkeys. Beautiful pheasants wandered about the manicured lawns. From time to time, we even cared for exotic animals such as flamingos.

I went to school at LaSalle of Miramar. We were school rivals with the Belen School of the Jesuits. I was a gentle, religious boy who had been spoiled and showered with love from "Mamicota" (great grandmother), "Maminena" (grandmother) and "Manina" (godmother). After Castro took power, life as a young exile would turn me harder.

Neither the Fowlers nor the Aguileras were involved in any way with the political situation. The upper class viewed the dictator Fulgencio Batista as a corrupt little thug with no class. They ignored Batista and Batista ignored them. By and large, Batista did not mess with Cuba's upper class. It wasn't in his interest to do so; he could make money off the mobsters and American businessmen. I will give you an example. Batista had a home near the Jenkins family in Varadero Beach. The Jenkins became my in-laws. My father-in-law, Eduardo Jenkins, told me a story about Batista. Batista was walking on a dock that extended into the beautiful Varadero Beach waters off the Club Kawama when Batista, with two armed bodyguards and fully dressed with a coat and tie, jokingly pushed Mr. Jenkins into the water. Since Mr. Jenkins owned a dairy farm that supplied the milk to Varadero Beach, he referred to Mr. Jenkins as *El Lechero*, or the Milkman. At the time, Mr. Jenkins was wearing a bathing suit. He got up on the dock, laughed and had a conversation with Batista. Mr. Jenkins, a very strong man and not one to be pushed around, decided to continue the game, so he grabbed the dictator and threw him fully clothed off the dock into the water. Mr. Jenkins remembered that he waited with some anxiety as the bodyguards closed in on him. Then, fortunately, Batista stuck his head out of the water and thankfully laughed. Fidel Castro would not have found it funny. He is a paranoid personality that can't laugh at himself. He probably would have had Mr. Jenkins killed.

During these years, my mother and father both strongly suspected that Castro was a communist. They unsuccessfully urged my grandfather, George Fowler, and Julian Aguilera, to move their fortunes out of Cuba.

The only member of our family who embraced Fidelismo was my idealistic, handsome young uncle, Tío Alberto. My father and my grandfather were furious at him for supporting Castro and told him that he was a fool to do so. I remember the arguments in the sugar mill. But in truth my uncle, like millions of Cubans, really thought Fidel Castro was a good man.

Castro has successfully promoted the myth that his victory was attributed to the poor classes and the poor financial condition of Cuba. That is simply inconsistent with the statistics. In the 50s, Cuba was prosperous and one of the five most advanced countries in Latin America. Cuba's gross domestic product per capita was high, Cuban workers' wages were substantial, and the labor laws progressive. It was hard to fire a Cuban worker. The international labor organization noted that the average industrial salary in Cuba was the world's eighth highest in 1958 and the average agricultural wage was higher than many European countries. Cuba had a sizeable and growing middle class. That is not to say that Cuba did not have a significant percentage of its population in poverty, but it was probably the last country in Latin American that should have been expected to become a communist nation.

I tease my mother about our family having cocktail parties while Castro was fighting and winning military battles in the Sierra Maestra Mountains. However, I cannot in truth blame them because Castro simply lied about who he was.

It is true that Cubans of the upper class had the opportunity and duty to be more involved in the political world and didn't. They needed to have had a more active involvement in order to ensure a fair and democratic government. They chose to party. I cannot help but compare that situation to Louisiana where I have lived for the last thirty some years. In New Orleans, the upper class simply generally does not get involved in politics. They leave that to the likes of shady politicians like Governor Edwin Edwards, who just served ten years in prison for corruption. By and large, like in Havana of the 50's, New Orleans' upper class chooses a great lifestyle to the dirty world of politics. Therefore, with some clear exceptions, many of our politicians turned to corruption to enhance their paychecks.

LIFE IN VARADERO BEACH

MAMA LISE PROVIDED A BEAUTIFUL ACCOUNT OF VARADERO'S charms in her book, *La Zafra*. A more accurate description has never been written:

> Nothing should ever be written about Cuba without mentioning Varadero. There is a well-known saying: "See Naples and die"—this should be said about Varadero too. Without a doubt, it is one of the most beautiful beaches in the world.
>
> Cuba calls it her *"Playa Azul,"* or Blue Beach, and indeed it is well named because its waters are of every shade of blue known to man.
>
> Mexico has Acapulco, Brazil boasts its Copacabana, Chile on the other coast its lovely Viña del Mar, and South Africans think there is nothing like Durban, but Varadero puts them all to shame in its untouched beauty. Artists come from all over to paint its seascapes, only to leave disheartened—fully convinced that it was a greater hand than that of man who mixed the colors blended together on this tiny spot of Cuba's Northern Shore.
>
> The sand is as white and powdery as new-fallen snow. The sand slopes gently to the water's edge, where a mad

symphony of blues begin. The colors are forever changing, every moment of the day. Far out on the horizon, the
water is indigo. This blends into a paler blue that, near-
er still, becomes turquoise; from there it is green as little
lacy waves race each other to the gleaming sand.

Sunrise in Varadero puts on glorious pageants.
During my stay there, I would often get up at dawn in
order to have this beautiful hour to myself. The sea is like
glass, not a ripple on the water, not a sound is heard, and
a perfect blending of every shade of blue and green.

By noon, a breeze comes up and white caps dot the
Gulf. When the sun begins to set, the zenith of beauty is
reached. The entire western sky turns pink, which causes the water to take on shades of deep purple and laven-
der. The white sands turn to gold, and the palms show
black against the sky. I never tired of looking at this wonderful color scheme. Varadero lies about sixty miles East
of Havana. It is reached by plane or a nice motor drive.

Spring and fall are the best seasons. The summer
crowd of noisy Cubans has not yet arrived, nor have the
droves of American tourists getting their winter tans.

My first visit caught me at the height of the Summer
Season. I arrived late in July for Regatta week. This
sleepy little town, which had been quietly basking in the
tropical sun for almost a year, suddenly wakes up and
puts on festive attire. It makes itself ready to welcome,
royally, a flock of young athletes who come there to row
for the National Cup of Cuba, a most coveted prize. The
President of Cuba presents the cup to the lucky crew, and
half of Cuba comes to see the competition.

Beautiful summer homes are crowded with guests.
Parties are in full swing and everyone who owns a place,
large or small, opens its doors and finds some little room

or corner where an extra cot can be squeezed in.

Hotels are packed; the few rooms available at the Yacht Club have been practically turned into dormitories for the young people. The swank Kawama Club has been booked up for weeks. The sky is the limit for rates at this time; nobody asks and nobody cares what they pay for this one weekend.

Havana society flocks in droves—the young crowd has waited all year for this event.

Five streamlined, shiny black shells are coming down to race for the President's Cup, each manned by its Club's best crewmen. The Cubans call this the Race of the Big Five. They are the Havana Yacht Club, the Biltmore Club, and the Vedado Tennis Club from Havana. The City of Cienfuegos sends a boat and little Varadero, herself, races in her home waters.

The crewmen, accompanied by their coaches and substitutes, have arrived a few days before in order to put in some last-minute training. This race always takes place the third Sunday of July, at eight o'clock in the morning.

By Friday afternoon the town begins to fill up. People arrive by motor, biplane, bus, and train. By Saturday the town is overflowing with young and old, brimming with excitement.

To me the most interesting crowd by far is the floating population—those who are brave enough to come by water. Every kind of craft imaginable has been put into commission and is made usable.

My two eldest boys were coming down from Havana with a crowd of young people, on our boat. I had motored down from "Narcisa" with my three girls. We arrived on Friday and no sooner settled ourselves in Kawama then the "floating" population began to arrive.

From the balcony of our rooms, overlooking the sea, we could see a steady stream of pleasure boats of all shapes and sizes coming from the West. Pretty yachts, bearing the pennant of their Club, slick little speedboats, puffing by the slower craft and leaving a track of water ripples behind them. Some would drop anchor at Kawama, and others would go to tie up at the Yacht Club. It looked as if all of Havana was on its way to Varadero.

For two hours, the girls and I anxiously watched this water pageant with sky glasses, recognizing, now and then, a familiar boat. At last I spotted the *Narcisa*, tossed about like a cork on the water, and, at this sight, my heart gave a little thump of gratefulness. My boys were safe. For nineteen years our good old *Narcisa* had tossed us mercilessly upon these waters, sometimes misbehaving quite badly, but like all good faithful boats, it finally made her port. She had not failed us.

Saturday night is the big night. By then everyone has arrived, and the hotels and bars are packed. The Yacht Club hoists up its gay pennants and opens its door to all visiting Clubs. Main Street is jammed, and there is a street fair going on with music and dancing in the street.

The town doesn't possess many taxis, but it does have the most wonderful collection of old, dilapidated Victorias that one could wish to ride in, and on the eventful night, they do a thriving business. Each one is loaded down with "young people" doing the town. "The Coachmen" use bicycle bells to scatter away the crowds, and the poor little underfed horses staggered bravely with their happy cargoes. This is a pre-celebration of tomorrow's race; everybody is sure that their favorite team will be victorious.

It is a big night indeed, and little Varadero is playing

host to the whole island of Cuba. But while all of this gaiety is going on, the principals of tomorrow's big event are nowhere to be seen.

The crews are practically jailed by their coaches. For months they have undergone strenuous training: no drinks, no cigarettes, early to bed, and early to rise has been their rule. Tonight they have been fed an early dinner of thick juicy steaks and sent, like little schoolboys, off to bed.

Regatta Sunday finds everybody up at dawn. In fact, few have even gotten to bed. At six-thirty, the little white church rings its bells loudly for the "*Misa de Remeros*," or the Oarsmen's Mass. Its hard, narrow benches are crowded with young girls from all over. The elder women puff and steam and fan and complain about the entire affair. The Church looks like a flower garden in the spring. Bright flowered kerchiefs "*à la Babush*" about the chins. Some wear a hibiscus or a wild orchid in their hair, some a black lace mantilla of old Spain, but one and all wear slacks. That seems to be the order of the day, and the Church grants its full permission, but only on Remero's Sunday.

At first I was a bit shocked to see slacks, painted toenails, and such in Church, but the wise old Padre closes his eyes to this once a year. The "*Misa de Remeros*" occurs not only in Varadero. When one of the Regattas takes place in Havana, the same thing is done at the Yacht Club. As the crew must get off so early, the Priest comes to the Club to say Mass. The big Ball Room is used as a Chapel. Everybody goes to Mass, the crew, the members, the servants of the Club, maids and waiters—nobody misses Mass on Regatta Sunday.

And now, no sooner is the last "Ave Maria" said, there

is a mad rush for the door, then a race to gobble down a cup of good coffee and to find a place to see the race. Of course, everybody who can tries to get on somebody else's boat, but all are not so fortunate and the beach offers a good viewpoint.

We hurried to the dinghy, which then rowed us out to the *Narcisa*. By that time, my girls and boys had collected about eighteen young people. Every few minutes, a friend from Havana was discovered and the invitation given: "Come along we have plenty of room!" I wondered how long our boat would stay afloat with such a list of passengers.

Our captain, knowing my weakness, brought me a steaming cup of coffee—and the feeling that I could now face the day. I armed myself with an enormous sun hat and some dark glasses, and then settled down to the stern role of chaperone to some twenty young girls and boys whose excitement knew no bounds. We were soon underway to reach a good spot near the goal.

My worries were not over. It was natural that the young people all gathered on one side of the boat in order to see the canoes, and I had visions of capsizing. It was useless to persuade them to divide themselves equally on both sides, so I moved my deck chair and sat quietly on an empty deck, looking at an empty horizon, feeling that I was evening up the balance. However, I soon realized that my one hundred fifteen pounds were doing absolutely no good and I was missing lots of fun, so I moved back to the popular side again. We found an excellent place to anchor, and now a really wonderful sight met our eyes.

Hundreds of pleasure boats had dropped anchor opposite the Yacht Club; it was a scene of big confusion.

Boats of all kinds were edging in to get a vantage point in the front places. One could easily recognize one's friends, carry on conversations, and make last-minute bets.

The Judges, accompanied by the Commodores of the five Big Clubs, now appeared in a little speed boat, followed by newspaper reporters, photographers, and, behind, the life-saving crew with all its doctors and equipment.

In the distance, five narrow shells could be seen trying to get into line. The crew of each wears its particular colors. There is difficulty getting a start, as the current is swift and the boats are like restless racehorses waiting to dash off. From the distance, the shells on the water look like five giant centipedes.

A shot is heard and they are off. From a distance, we keep in step with the other boats following the race. As the shells near the goal, the excitement grows. Shouting spectators cheering on their favorite crews. We follow with spyglasses, passing them from one to another.

We have bet on the Havana Yacht Club, and it is gaining now—but one cannot tell as sometimes the last shell comes in first. It is anybody's race.

Seven interminable minutes lapse until the goal is passed. The Yacht Club has won!

A deafening din is now heard as everybody shouts and sings; the boats all blow their sirens. It is like New Year's Eve concentrated into a few seconds. Hats and caps are thrown into the air. A favorite outlet for pent-up emotions seems to be jumping overboard. Boys and girls laugh and cry and kiss each other. Latin temperaments know no bounds at this time.

The scene on the Beach is every bit as exciting as what happens on the boats. The Yacht Club is black with people. Balconies, windows, and even the roof haven't even standing room. The wide stretch of beach in front is a mass of humanity, all waving and shouting.

Crowds now rush to the water's edge and pull the exhausted crews from their shells, giving way to the victors to be carried on their shoulders into the Club.

The President is waiting to present the trophy, the band strikes up the strain of the National Anthem, and the ceremony is over.

But now the real fun begins. First there is breakfast with dancing, lunch with dancing, dinner with dancing, and more dancing until the sun sets and the weary but happy crowds realize that all fun must end and that it is time to get back to their homes.

Little by little the big yachts get under way, followed by a trail of satellites. The crowds disperse; cars and packed buses all find their way to the highway and start for home.

The town empties itself. Main Street becomes dark and deserted. The *Regatta* is over. Varadero settles herself for another lazy year.

The turquoise waves lap gently against the white sand. The noonday sun blazes mercilessly down on the Gulf, and the setting sun reflects its ever-changing colors on the sparkling sea. Man has come and man has gone, leaving this beautiful little spot untouched and unspoiled. She is as fair as ever.

THE RISE OF FIDEL CASTRO

IT IS NOT HARD TO FIND THE ORIGIN OF FIDEL CASTRO'S ANGER towards America and the upper classes. It is rooted in his early life and fueled by envy.

Fidel's father, Ángel Castro y Argiz, was a relatively wealthy landowner from Galicia, Spain. Ángel moved to the Oriente Province in Cuba to work in the sugar industry, where he had to pander to the Americans of the United Fruit Company to help his business. After Ángel divorced his first wife, he began a relationship with his housemaid, Lina Ruz González. Born out of wedlock, Castro was their third child of five, Raúl being the youngest.

This formed the basis of his personal hatred for Cuba's upper class. He would get to know them well at Belen, the Jesuit High School in Havana. His classmates knew about his illegitimate background and Cuba's high society was not tolerant. Castro knew he was not accepted. He became obsessed with power and sought to exact his revenge in spades.

However, his Jesuit education made a strong impression on Castro. He was an athlete and a debater with a prodigious memory. There is no questioning Castro's intelligence. He is brilliant, manipulative, and resourceful. He read *Mein Kampf* and Lenin's *What Is To Be Done*.[5] According to his brother Raúl, "*He*

---

[5] Hugh Thomas, *Cuba or the Pursuit of Freedom* (De Capo Press, 1988), p. 807.

succeeded in everything. In sport, in study. And everyday he fought. He had a very explosive nature. He defied the most powerful and the strongest and when he was beaten, he began again the next day. He never gave up."[6]

In October, 1945, Castro went to the University of Havana and chose to study law. At the university, he was known as a thug who carried a gun and killed a student leader in cold blood. Because of his unkempt appearance, he was nicknamed *dirtball*. From day one, Castro spent his time in political activity. His friends were members of the communist youth.

As strange as it may seem, elections in student politics at the University of Havana were decided by fights and guns. Castro was a *dirtball* of fire. He was endlessly conspiring for leadership positions at the university and involved in gangster style wars. In the middle of his law studies, he participated in the famous *Bogotazo*. In April, 1948, a Pan American conference was set to be held in Bogota, the capital of Colombia, to reform the old Pan American union of American states into what became the Organization of American States. The United States sent General Marshall as its representative. Castro and some other Cuban and Argentinean students traveled to Bogota to disrupt the event. They succeeded. The demonstrations resulted in the death of a much loved Colombian leader, Jorge Eliecer Gaitan. Gaitan was the hope for Colombian social reform. After Gaitan's murder, Castro came on the radio and said, "This is Fidel Castro from Cuba. This is a communist revolution. The president has been killed, all the military establishments in Colombia are now in our hands, the navy has capitulated to us and this revolution has been a success."[7]

This was mostly false, but it gives you a good idea of who Fidel Castro was.

---

[6] Hugh Thomas, *Cuba or the Pursuit of Freedom* (De Capo Press, 1988), p. 808.
[7] Hugh Thomas, *Cuba or the Pursuit of Freedom*, p. 816.

Castro never enjoyed a normal life. He married, but his life seemed to revolve around politics and power. His life as a lawyer was short and inconsequential. He really did not know how to make a living, nor did he care to do so. After the unsuccessful July 26, 1953, *Moncada* attack on November 25, 1956, Castro set sail from Veracruz with eighty-one revolutionaries to begin his revolution in Cuba in earnest. The ship was called the *Granma* and it is now the name of his newspaper in Cuba. From time to time, they write about me in not so favorable terms.

From the jungle, Castro, Che Guevara, and Camilo Cienfuegos attacked small army posts to obtain weapons. Locals joined them although most new recruits came from the cities. In 1957, Castro divided his army into three columns, giving one to his brother, Raúl, and the other one to Che Guevara. Throughout Cuba, Castro supporters were rising up against Batista, carrying out bombings and other acts of subversion. At this time Castro, deep in the Sierra Maestra Mountains, received invaluable help from *The New York Times* through the reporter, Herbert Matthews, who turned Castro into a world celebrity. Castro was and is still wonderful copy. On November, 1958, Castro's forces controlled Las Villas and Oriente provinces and were close to controlling the capitals of Santiago and Santa Clara. Eventually by controlling Las Villas, where the Fowlers' sugar mill was (and where he got help from Tío Alberto), Castro succeeded in dividing Cuba in two to the disadvantage of Batista's military. Batista was on his way out.

In 1958, Cuba's entire population seemed pro-Castro with few exceptions, my mother and father being among those. They saw Castro for what he was, an egocentric communist. I am sure there were many others feeling the same, but that certainly was not what I heard on the streets. As a little boy, everywhere I went there was talk of Fidel Castro and it was joyful, hopeful talk.

JANUARY 1, 1959
CASTRO TAKES CUBA

I WOKE UP TO THE SOUND OF MULTIPLE SHOTS. THESE WERE no New Year's firecrackers. The house was filled with commotion. I was told that Batista had fled the country on a plane bound for Santo Domingo. Cuba was in Castro's hands. The rebels had won.

The TV reported the rounding up of the *Batistianos*, Batista's supporters. In quiet whispers, I heard the word *paredón* (the wall) for the first time. People were being taken to *el paredón* and shot—no trials.

I could tell my mother was troubled, but she stayed quiet throughout the tumult. She and Father had been at a big New Year's Eve party at the home of a Batistiano, Fernando de la Riva, who had run away upon hearing of Batista's departure.

Our maids excitedly received visitors, "*los milicianos*"—the militia. Young men came into the house sporting long black beards and clean green fatigues. They wore the same attire as Castro and his rebels on the TV, but these guys didn't look dirty or tired. That day, everybody in Cuba claimed to have been a soldier in Castro's revolution. The *milicianos* flirted with our maids and bragged about their exploits; they proudly showed me their rifles and large caliber bullets. I sensed they were full of it.

In the days after Batista fled, I experienced hatred fueled by class envy for the first time. Every Thursday, my great-grandfather would let the poor kids into Villa Viejo's gardens. They had thirty minutes to gather as many fruits, mangoes, oranges, and avocados as they could. I had always played with them and helped them pick the best fruits. They seemed to like me; after all, I was a boy just like them. Shortly after Castro took power, I left Villa Viejo with Mamicota in her chauffeured black Cadillac. Those same poor kids were there, and I cheerfully waved at them. But some threw rocks at the car and grimaced at me menacingly. They seemed to hate me. I felt confused and sad.

As I look back and try to analyze what went on, I realize that although I had a strong personal affection for the good people who worked in my house and in Villa Viejo, no doubt they had rightfully dreamt of financial equality. Castro's promises that he was going to take away from the wealthy and give to the poor must have resonated strongly in their ears. I can assure you that no time did I see any kind of mistreatment or disrespect in my home or in Villa Viejo. The same was true for the workers of the sugar mill who were very kind to me when I visited their *bohios*[8] in Narcisa's lands. The relationship between our family and these people was warm and genuine. As exiles, my family, particularly my sister Lita and my cousin Elizabeth Swanson, have gathered money from our family to help some of our former household help and workers in the sugar mill. We have sensed no anger, just the contrary. Their letters to us recall good memories and friendship. They feel they were betrayed by Castro also.

Once while in Miami in 2001, after a disagreeable meeting with U.S. Attorney General Ashcroft wherein I asked that he indict Fidel Castro for the Brothers to the Rescue Murders, I was being driven by a taxi to the airport. I asked the driver if he had heard in the news about my meeting with Ashcroft. He at

---

[8]A *bohio* is the thatched roofed home of the Cubans who live in the country.

first didn't answer and then surprisingly, pulled over on LeJeune Road, 42nd Avenue. He stopped the car, turned around and said to me "you are George Fowler, are you not?" I told him that I was. He teared up and said that he and his thirteen brothers and sisters worked for the Fowlers at the sugar mill in Narcisa. He said that he would gladly trade in his taxicab (which he had worked hard to purchase) if he could go back and work for the Fowlers in Narcisa and ride a mule. Then it was I who started tearing up. He told me that the Fowlers had built homes for them and that whenever they needed anything they would just ask them for it. He specifically remembered Tío Alberto for his generosity. Tío Alberto was the world's worst businessman. I am sure, were it not for the oversight of his father, he would have given the entire sugar mill away to the workers. His love was for the land, but more so for its people. I feel the same way.

As far as the poor boys in Villa Viejo, I am sure that some were consumed with envy and I have little tolerance for that. I am also sure that many of them did not hate me.

As a little boy, I was pro-Castro. I believed in the revolution and was part of the jubilant mood that engulfed our island. At LaSalle School, we began to collect stickers with the pictures of the top generals of the revolution. We traded them as if they were baseball cards before licking them and putting them in a scrapbook. There were thirty-three so-called leaders, but four of the stickers were the most valuable: Fidel, Camilo Cienfuegos, Che Guevara, and Raúl Castro.

Camilo was handsome, with fine features and a long black beard. He sported a cowboy hat and had an easy smile. He exuded charisma and was well loved by the people. Camilo was not a communist and made his views known to Fidel. His strong personality cast a shadow over Castro.

Unfortunately for Camilo, in Castro's Cuba, only one man can shine. In October 1959, Cienfuegos disappeared in his plane. Even as a nine-year-old, I heard rumors that Castro had killed him. Years later, Che Guevara—another man who had a larger-than-life image in Cuba—chose to leave rather than face a similar fate. He, too, was killed while promoting a communist insurrection in Bolivia.

Tío Alberto became friends with Camilo and helped him lead the rebel forces in Santa Clara. To the chagrin of my grandfather and father, Tío helped Cienfuegos build a makeshift tank in the sugar mill and supplied him with guns.

Tío Alberto was mischievous. He and another of my uncles, Dr. Juan Weiss, told me a story often repeated in family reunions. Juan, who was married to my aunt Lisette, was a dentist and a formidable tennis player—he was Cuba's tennis champion and went to the Davis Cup seven times. Since he didn't like dentistry and was familiar with cattle, he chose to work with the Fowlers at the sugar mill. He was responsible for taking care of our *cebú*, a breed of cattle that has a large hump. Mostly, though, Juan played tennis. One of Juan's best friends, Andres Perez Chaumont, was a Batista General. Andres captured Fidel after the assault on the Moncada barracks in 1953, but unfortunately let him go.

One evening, Tío Alberto asked Juan to accompany him to town from the sugar mill. Juan agreed, not knowing what was in store for him. As they were driving, Tío Alberto abruptly cut into the cane fields and drove through them to a clearing, where Castro's *milicianos* surrounded the car. Juan was fearful because of his well-known Batista contacts. Tío Alberto opened the trunk pulled out a cache of weapons for the *milicianos*. Tío Alberto was laughing, but poor Uncle Juan was petrified and yelled at him the whole way back to the mill.

Castro's revolution was a success because of the help he got from the upper and middle class. Nobody wanted Batista—but they had no idea what they were getting into with Fidel. There was little immediate impact on my family after the revolution. We kept on as before, but my mother and father began making plans to leave the country. The social life continued, but now there was palpable fear and trepidation. As Castro began to arrest, first the Batistianos and thereafter the wealthy, people became nervous. There were fewer parties and more whispering. The discussion of politics was prohibited in my home. We were taking no chances.

THE KILLINGS BEGIN

FIDEL CASTRO FINALLY ENTERED HAVANA ON JANUARY 8, 1959. The church bells rang as cannons went off. Nobody can stage a scene like Fidel. Some say he should have been a major league ballplayer—I say he should have been a movie director. He gave his triumphant victory speech at Camp Colombia's headquarters. From time to time, he would stop, turn to Camilo, and ask, "*Voy bien, Camilo?*" ("Am I doing all right, Camilo?") As if he needed anybody's approval.

Here he announced his program to strip the population of weapons: "*¿Armas para Que?*" ("Why do we need weapons?") Now we know that it was so only his army would have guns. The population was made defenseless.

He gave notice that *el paredón* would soon be put to use. Once the killings started, no law, no judge could save you. And so it is today. People without weapons cannot free themselves from a brutal dictator. This year, Castro will celebrate fifty-four years in power. He has been in the *Guinness Book of World Records* as the world's longest-ruling dictator for many years.

I watched Castro's memorable televised speech where two white doves flew and then perched on his shoulders. The crowds called out his name. Fidel was blessed by the Almighty—or so they thought. The magazine *Bohemia* portrayed Castro as

Christ-like. Castro was an atheist, but because Cubans by and large were Catholics, he manipulated his public image to look like Jesus. He is like a chameleon in that way. In reality, Fidel's pact is with the Devil, and both have kept their part of the bargain.

Castro came down from the mountains with a crucifix, proclaiming that he was a Christian and denying he was a communist. It was only a year later, when he was totally in control, that he revealed his communist sympathies. He put out a slogan: "*Si Fidel es comunista, ponme en la lista.*" ("If Fidel is a communist, put me on the list.") After his slogan caught on, he declared himself a Marxist-Leninist and started confiscating properties and businesses.

The old Spanish forts—El Morro, La Cabaña, San Severino, and others—provided the dungeons where Castro's thugs tortured and killed those deemed enemies of the revolution. In Cuba, there exists a law today called *La Ley de La Peligrosidad*. This law permits the imprisonment of anybody who presents a "danger" to the *revolución*. In the early days, the law was applied quite liberally; many innocent people were indiscriminately arrested, imprisoned, tortured, and killed.

Castro had thousands of Batista's men sentenced to death at kangaroo court hearings and "revolutionary tribunals." The trials were broadcast on TV. I remember watching the trial of Major Jesús Sosa Blanco, a brave man who accused his judges of acting like a "mob." He was executed notwithstanding a brave defense. There were chants on the street calling for Sosa Blanco to be sent to the firing squad. *Uno, dos, tres, cuatro, que maten a Sosa Blanco* (one, two, three, four, kill Sosa Blanco). My future wife, Cristina, was punished by her mother for chanting this rhyme; she didn't realize she was singing for someone's death.

In March 1959, Fidel demanded a new trial for forty-four aviators from Batista's army. The jury had acquitted them because they were military men simply following orders. Fidel got what he asked for, and the aviators were convicted. Fidel has no sense of justice; he ignores the principle of "innocent until proven guilty" and kills at will.

Most Cuban exiles have a family member or friend who lost their life to Castro's cruelty. One example is my good friend José Suquet, another Cuban American success story. Also based in New Orleans, he has helped me to correct misimpressions about Castro by our media. I never tell them what they want to hear, but the New Orleans Cubans tell the reporters to talk to me.

José tells them about the cowardly execution of his uncle, Colonel Armando Suárez Suquet. The Colonel was the fiercest Castro foe in Batista's army, and his men were well trained and effective. He relentlessly pursued the rebels—or "rats," as he called them—and came just short of capturing Che Guevara, who barely escaped to Las Villas.

After Castro won, the Colonel hid in the mountains to continue the fight. After waging a bold guerilla campaign, he was captured and tortured by Castro's forces. He was a tall, handsome man, but unfortunately, he was also a diabetic. He grew sick without his medication, but his guards refused to administer insulin and sent him into a diabetic coma. José told me they wheeled him to *el paredón* and shot him while unconscious, the rats.

Raúl Castro and Che Guevara were no better. Raúl was a cold-blooded murderer who personally and enthusiastically executed the political prisoners in La Cabaña Fortress with his handgun. He is known as an effete, mentally unstable alcoholic who killed for pleasure. Raúl is feared in Cuba, but not like Fidel. Fidel never respected Raúl and once made him cry in the mountains after a fight. *El Che* was just as vicious, but crazy in a different way; he was a communist who accepted murder as part of his mandate.

Mother told me that during this period, many of their friends were imprisoned and some of them shot. She told me that she had to restrain my father, who was known to throw a punch, from fighting with people who no longer respected anyone. They felt that because Castro had taken over, they did not have to respect others, particularly those of the upper class. She told me that more than once she had to break up a fight because my father would not accept disrespect.

My grandfather, George Fowler, lost the Narcisa sugar mill to Castro's confiscatory policies. He decided he would go see Che Guevara, who had been appointed head of the Cuban National Bank. He was given an appointment but was not able to see El Che until three in the morning. He was forced to wait for hours. It's a communist tactic to weaken the opposition. My grandfather offered his services to run the confiscated sugar mill for free for the revolution. El Che told him that he should leave his office before he shot him.

The U.S. State Department records reveal the developing situation in Cuba:[9]

As of January 14, 1959:
Document 225 – Revolutionary Justice
Events in Oriente – Reaction (January 6-14, 1959)
Following consolidation of the provisional government in Santiago, the new authorities began an immediate roundup of persons believed to have been responsible for deaths and other crimes during the former regime. The names of nearly three hundred persons arrested appeared in the newspapers and the total property seized although many have been released. Seventy were reported shot in Santiago (one of the seventy-one was supposedly freed). While rebels have long announced that they

[9] U.S. Department of State, Office of the Historian, Foreign Relations of the United States, 1958-1960, Vol. VI, Cuba.Doc. 257.

would take drastic action against "criminals," the action has left some doubt in a few minds. Despite minor thoughts and minor disapprovals, the general public feels that those responsible for murder should be eliminated.

There are stories that not all persons receive a full dress court-martial, and that in some cases the formalities were pretty much limited to sentencing. ...all those executed were supposedly persons about whom there were "no doubts" as to guilt. It is generally stated that they were all participants in murder or tortures or responsible for them. ... the murders presumably followed hurried investigation of many alleged killings and tortures by agents of the government. Details of crimes are being brought to light and the bodies of persons long missing are supposedly being removed, recovered from wells, sewers, military installations and isolated spots throughout the province. ...the startling quantity of people executed at once has undoubtedly left a bad taste with a few, but none will admit that there are not others who need to be treated the same.

Protests from the press of the United States and elsewhere seem to be disregarded with the rationalization that the United States took no notice whatsoever with the crimes and atrocities committed under the previous regime when there was not even a pretense of legal formalities.[10]

As of February 25, 1959:

Some prisoners now may be, and are, indefinitely held without charge. In their zeal to eradicate all traces of the corruption and repression previous regime, the authorities are engaging in some of the practices they most objected to. In Camaguey on February 11, local

[10] U.S. Department of State, Office of the Historian, Foreign Relations of the United States, 1958-1960, Vol. VI, Cuba.Doc. 225.

persons estimated that there were about 1,000 persons in jail, under extremely crowded conditions, most of whom were being held without charge. This more than doubled the highest figure recorded under Batista. An American citizen has been held in prison by the "26 of July" Movement and the new government since December 26, 1958, without charge. The civilian courts are being purged, and are only partly functioning. Revolutionary Courts, operating under the "rebel code of justice," conducting summary courts-martial of persons both civilian and military accused of a wide variety of crimes committed under the previous regime. Trials, particularly in the provinces, are often mere formalities. The accused is sometimes given the right of appeal. In Habana, appeals are heard by the same judge and the prosecutor who conducted the original trial.

The press has exercised self-censorship. No paper dares to appear to criticize the government or the leading figures of the new regime. Fidel Castro has displayed a very thin skin and deep resentment of criticism. He recently publicly objected to a cartoon in a weekly humorous publication. The staff of the publication explained in detail that no disrespect was intended, and published a deeply apologetic statement in the next issue —all this over a cartoon whose criticism was directed not at Castro, but rather at those who had been busily jumping on the revolutionary bandwagon since the first of the year.

Tío Alberto slowly came to the realization that Fidel Castro was not what he envisioned and that he was a communist. Fidel was not like his friend, Camilo. Tío Alberto told me that he immediately began to plot against him and joined counter revolutionary forces. They were tracking him in Havana so he mounted his beautiful black horse, Carioca, and rode it to the sugar mill, a ten hour train ride away. He said it took him five days to get to the sugar mill and was shot at several times. In Narcisa, he found that the situation was just as dangerous for him. Castro had a firm control on the mill and was looking for Tío Alberto. Tío Alberto eventually escaped Cuba and joined the Bay of Pigs invaders.

THE AMERICAN WHO REFUSED TO TAKE A KNEE

ONE MAN WHO REFUSED TO BEND A KNEE TO THE DICTATOR was William Alexander Morgan—the *Yankee Comandante* (the American Commander). A true American hero, Morgan was murdered by a firing squad on March 11, 1961—two years after he had helped overthrow Batista and bring Castro to power. He was the only American in the rebel army and the sole foreigner—other than Guevara, an Argentine—to rise to its highest rank, *Comandante*.

After seeing the horrors of the *revolución*, Morgan voiced his opposition to Castro's violent regime. Jealous of Morgan's power, Castro charged the Yankee with conspiring to overthrow him. Morgan was arrested and moved to La Cabaña, a prison fortress that overlooked Havana Harbor. He underwent the usual kangaroo court and was sentenced to death.

Morgan prayed the whole way to *el paredón*; he removed his rosary and gave it to a priest, asking that his mother receive it. Through the spotlights, Morgan peered at the muzzles of the rifles. One of Castro's thugs yelled, "Kneel, *and beg for your life.*"

Morgan replied, "*I kneel for no man.*" One of the cowardly executioners then shot him in the right knee. The American Commander refused to kneel; he stayed on his feet as blood spilled around him. Then they shot him in the left knee. Finally, he collapsed and was repeatedly shot in the head and body. According to one witness, his head was "blown off." Many of the men there who witnessed the tragedy broke into tears.

My father-in-law, Eduardo, often told me this story. The big man's eyes would water as he remembered the brave American who loved Cuba; he would try to hide his emotions by coughing. Half the time, he was unable to finish the story of the *Yankee Comandante*'s courage.

THE FOWLERS FLEE CUBA

AT HOME, MOTHER MADE IT CLEAR SHE WAS NOT A SUPPORTER of Fidel. Seeing the cold blooded murders and the property confiscations, my parents decided to leave Cuba. I was told to keep this a secret as we prepared to leave. On May 17, 1960, Mother, Father, my older sister Lita, my little sister Lisette, and I boarded a Pan American flight and left Cuba for Miami. I have never returned, but as the Cuban exile song says, I "left my heart buried there."

We were not the only ones. Over the years, approximately one million people fled the country, some on inner tubes and makeshift rafts in shark infested waters. To put that in perspective, Cuba's population in 1959 was seven million people.

I was told that we would return to Cuba in a few days, but I left everything behind—my dog Chicha, my home, my grandparents, my great-grandparents, and Villa Viejo. I remember being draped in women's jewelry under my clothes—you could only take what you were wearing; the rest of your properties and assets were forfeited to Castro when you left.

It was a sad moment for my family, but for me, too young to understand, it was an adventure. I had never been on a plane and wanted to enjoy it. My older sister, Lita, knew better and asked me to pray the rosary.

Those first few days in the United States were wonderful for me, although I felt guilty because I knew I was supposed to be sad. We stayed at a fabulous hotel in Miami, the Miami Villas. There, for the first time, I heard an argument about money. My mother was furious at my father for booking a hotel room that cost $90 per night. For the first time in our lives, we had little money. Our grandparents disapproved of us leaving Cuba and cut my father off and he had no personal wealth. From there we went to a less expensive hotel, the Escape Hotel in Fort Lauderdale, where I swam in the lit pool at night with my sisters as my father drank martinis with his friends.

We stayed in Fort Lauderdale for two years. I entered the fifth grade at Bayview Elementary and was taught by a nice blonde lady named Mrs. Christiansen. I knew how to take advantage of her; whenever she asked me a homework question, I would say, "No spickity English," and she would move on. One day, she heard me talking baseball slang with the other boys on the field, and the jig was up. In two months, I spoke flawless English—cuss words and all.

Shortly after I arrived in the city, my mother told me to get a job since we had no money, and I started selling the *Miami News* in Fort Lauderdale for ten cents a paper. At the time, I thought Americans were stupid businesspeople because my boss told me I could keep the whole dime. I later realized that they were just trying to introduce the Miami News to the city. It was hard work; most of the time people rejected me, and I was kicked out of many a store.

But I persisted. I pretended not to speak English, and soon the shop owners in our neighborhood took pity on me—or just got tired of me—and bought my paper. After only a month, I became the top salesman. In my most memorable professional achievement, I was taken to ride go-carts. I was proud; I felt like I had learned to be an American.

One day, my great-grandmother, Mamicota, the former mistress of Villa Viejo, accidentally ran into me selling papers on the street. She was devastated and said we had hit rock-bottom. Later, I found her weeping in our little apartment on Middle River Drive. I tried to console her by telling her the truth: I was elated to be free and making my own money. After all, the rich doctor's kid that lived next door delivered newspapers, too. After selling twelve newspapers, I could buy a Superman comic book—I was in love with Lois Lane and Lana Lang—and a Nestlé Crunch bar. Ever the salesman, I told her she could help me by buying whatever newspapers I couldn't sell. She did, too—she was the sweetest woman on the planet.

This was my first of thirty-six menial jobs I held until I became a lawyer. I was proud of every one of them. I thrived in democratic, capitalist America, never feeling poor or sorry for myself. For me, work was always a liberating pleasure. My older sister felt otherwise; she had been the little princess of Villa Viejo and sorely felt the loss of her lifestyle.

My mother, a tough woman, made ends meet and got a job selling dresses. Regrettably, my father drank too much and couldn't hold down a job. Although she had some money saved up, my father would squander it on speculative business ventures. He started a business called E-Z Roll to move washing machines, refrigerators, and such. The business failed.

It all became too much for my mother. In 1961, when I was eleven years old, she decided to get a divorce. My father asked me to convince her not to divorce him, but I told him that it was not my business. I wasn't going to second-guess my mother—I knew she would take care of us no matter what. She did then, and she still does now.

After the divorce, my father moved to Panama and got a job with Merrill Lynch, Pierce & Fenner. He took his life later that year. Although I rationalized his death and moved on, as we have had to do to survive, the truth is that it has been a heavy load to bear. I am not nearly as tough as I would like to be. I feel sorry for my dad. He never achieved what his personal talents promised. He never got to meet his wonderful grandchildren and great-grandchildren. When I was about fourteen, I traveled to Palm Beach to visit my grandfather George, who was devastated. He told me he should have paid more attention to my father and treated him better. Mother always told me that she never would have gotten a divorce if she had stayed in Cuba.

My grandfather, George Fowler, had lost Narcisa to Castro's confiscatory laws. When he tried to leave Cuba on his yacht Narcisa II, which he had filled with art and other valuables, Castro had also taken possession of the Narcisa II. He found out about this upon arrival at the dock.

Very few Cubans ended up in Fort Lauderdale, the vast majority went to Miami. My family went to Fort Lauderdale because our grandfather had moved to Fort Lauderdale. He got a job as the general manager of a yacht resort called Bahia Mar which is still there. The owner was a female friend of his from his yachting days. Castro had stolen the Narcisa II.

Our family's exile is not unlike thousands of others. I can tell you that with few exceptions the Cuban exile families that I know are good examples of American values. They cherish their family, have a strong work ethic and are survivors. They began sweeping banks and became the owners of banks. I ended up at LSU where I met my wife, Cristina, and married her when I was twenty-one. We had a class reunion of the Cuban Club of LSU thirty years later and virtually every one of the 300 students was married to his/her first spouse and had good, loving families. They were all successes in one form or the other. Many had formed large corporations that created significant employment. Some were successes in medicine, architecture, literature, theatre and the arts. In New Orleans, we have a men's luncheon club and we call ourselves the Mambo Kings. If you go to Antoine's you will see our picture. Fidel Castro drove out wonderful, talented people to the benefit of the United States and to the detriment of Cuba.

The Bay of Pigs Fiasco

In April 1960, John Kennedy gave the go-ahead for the formation of the Bay of Pigs invasion force at the hands of the CIA. Known as Brigade 2506, the force was made up of Cuban men from a variety of social classes with one common desire— to free their homeland. When we first heard about the invasion, we were all elated. We were confident that we would win and that Castro would be deposed.

In the days preceding the Bay of Pigs invasion, my father and mother often argued. My father wanted to join the invaders and fight to free our country. My mother said that he needed to stay and support us—and he couldn't help the family if he was dead. He ultimately decided not to enlist. My uncle, Tío Alberto, disgusted with Castro's excesses, bravely joined the invasion force. Little did we know that the young, inexperienced, and timid President of the United States, John Kennedy, would abandon Tío and 1,500 of his brave comrades on the beaches of Cuba.

The invasion finally took place on April 17, 1961. My father had recently bought a musty old car for only $100. It barely ran, but it had a radio. I sat alone in that car for all four days, listening to every report on the radio and hoping for victory. At the beginning, the reports were euphoric. They soon turned sour. Those days were very difficult for me—I knew all too well that

Tío could be killed. Years later, Tío told me what happened. The invaders landed on the beach and fought bravely until they used up all their ammunition. Tío signaled the men on the American ships off the coast for help. He could see the military men on the ships with his binoculars. The Americans were obviously agitated to see their allies being decimated by the monster in Havana.

The U.S. government had promised to support the invading force. However, the carrier repeatedly refused Tío's requests for air cover. Help did not come. Castro's air force was supposed to have been destroyed before the invasion landing, but it remained intact. No support whatsoever came from the United States, although an aircraft carrier, the USS *Essex*, and six destroyers were present to watch the chaos unfold.

Tío fought with a bazooka, then with his sidearm, until he ran out of ammunition. He penetrated deep into the swamps of the Bay of Pigs, where he was met by one of Castro's captains. The officer wanted to join the invaders and asked where Tío's force was. Tío admitted that he was on his own. The captain chose to fight alongside Tío alone; he could not tell his men to join only one man. I don't know who that captain was, but he was a good man who fought until he was killed.

The invaders fought valiantly for their homeland. Tío said that for every casualty on the invasion force, ten of Castro's men were either killed or wounded. Cuba admitted to 1,250 dead and nearly 3,000 wounded. The inexperienced invaders of Brigade 2506 fought with their hearts.

At the end of the Eisenhower Administration, the Joint Chiefs of Staff appointed a committee to study the CIA's invasion plan. Among those who reviewed the plan were Dean Rusk, Robert McNamara and John Kennedy's brother, Robert. But the responsibility for the failure, a black mark on the history of our great country, falls squarely on the shoulders of John Kennedy.

The inexperienced John Kennedy put incompetent men in charge of the invasion force. The commanders spoke no Spanish and were contemptuous of the Cubans, treating them as if they were a band of ignorant peasants. In reality, many of those in the invasion force were far more educated than their American commanders. My uncle told me that some of the military trainers were arrogant and displayed a basic lack of common sense and intelligence.

The initial invasion training occurred in Guatemala. The American trainers were given the best accommodations and treated the Cuban trainees with disdain.

One of the U.S. commanders of the invasion force was one Richard Bissell of the CIA. Bissell had no knowledge of Cuban history, Cuban geography, or the Cuban people. He underestimated Fidel Castro. He was—like many involved in the disastrous operation—ignorant. It was no wonder the attack turned into such a fiasco. John Kennedy was so unschooled on Cuba that he actually sought the help of the Governor of Puerto Rico, Luis Muñoz Marin. I guess Kennedy assumed that because Muñoz Marin was Puerto Rican, he knew all about Cuba.

After the invasion failed, the invading Cubans were blamed for being disorganized and fighting with each other. Cubans are known for their stubbornness, but when the 1,500 men landed in the Bay of Pigs, they were united. They were one force. Cubans might be quarrelsome, but they are smart enough to know when to band together for a common purpose.

Kennedy wanted to have plausible deniability at all costs and was adamant about keeping the operation secret. Of course, his effort failed miserably. Cubans can't keep secrets. Even I, as a ten-year-old boy, knew when the attack would take place. The invasion was like something out of a *Keystone Cops* movie. Custer's attack at the Battle of Little Big Horn was like D-Day in comparison.

The original plan was for the landing force to invade the city of Trinidad, but Kennedy thought it would be "too spectacular." He wanted a "quiet" invasion. In other words, he wanted to overthrow a powerful regime—with an army of 500,000 trained men-at-arms—in a way that no one would know who did it.

Perhaps the most decisive factor in the invasion's failure was the leadership. Fidel Castro may have been a brutal dictator, but he was also a seasoned warrior with well-trained troops. Although he was ten years younger than the forty-three-year-old Kennedy, he was a battle-hardened veteran and knew the Cuban terrain like the back of his hand. Castro was decisive, and his men obeyed him. If they didn't, they died.

Meanwhile, John Kennedy was untested in that form of war. Less than a week before the invasion was scheduled to begin, John Kennedy hadn't even made up his mind whether or not to carry it out. Moreover, he issued news reports that suggested that the United States would not intervene in Cuba. The CIA even hired a public relations agency to issue publicity releases on behalf of the invasion force. The invaders needed weapons, airplanes, and proper training—not a PR agent.

The attack was a disaster. The U.S. military's promise to destroy Castro's air force was not kept, and Castro had all the air strength he needed—T33 trainer jets and Sea Furies—to keep the invaders at bay. Many of the landing boats got caught up on the reefs, so the men had to wade ashore through deep water.

Although the beach landing was initially successful, Castro used the national radio and television stations to advise the Cubans of the attack. The *milicianos* were ordered to take positions against the Americans. By the evening of April 17, Castro had mobilized 60,000 men, twenty long-range Soviet carriers, and forty tanks. Conversely, by the second day of the invasion, the only invasion vessel that carried fuel, ammunition, food, and medical supplies had been disabled.

On that second day, the reports on the radio gave me the impression that the rebel forces were winning. That evening, April 18, the Kennedys hosted a formal party at the White House. It must have been an unhappy night for President Kennedy. The CIA pleaded with him to use jet fighters to support the invasion force, but he refused. He refused to get "involved" in an operation that he planned, organized, and authorized. General Eisenhower wrote in his diary that the collapse at the Bay of Pigs was a "profile in timidity and indecision."

By the third day, it was obvious that the invasion had been a failure. I prayed hard for the lives of my uncle and the others. Tío hid in the Cuban countryside for several weeks and ultimately was captured after he was found hiding inside a well. 1,179 Bay of Pigs invaders were captured after running out of ammunition. One hundred were killed. The fate of the others is unknown. The Brigade 2506 never officially surrendered. After being abandoned by Kennedy, they simply ran out of bullets.

Castro's cruelty was evident from the beginning. In his boastful radio speeches, he bragged about destroying the *"gusanos,"* or worms, as he called all of us exiles. One of the insignias worn by the Bay of Pigs invaders was a cartoon figure of a worm with a gun—a playful take on the insult. Castro could call the invaders whatever he wanted; they would fight to the end regardless.

Under the directions of Commander Osmani Cienfuegos, brother of the popular Camilo Cienfuegos, the captured invaders were stuffed in trucks one on top of the other like pancakes. The men struggled to breathe through tiny holes in the metal, and nine of them died of suffocation. Jose Macias, a friend of my family, died in this inhumane way. Mother told me he was very handsome and flirted with her when he was young.

The 1,179 prisoners were rounded up and brought to the Sports Palace in Havana. Castro, who loved to show off and to be the center of attention, personally took over the interrogation of the invading force. Many of the men boldly spoke back. Castro confronted one of the invaders, who was black, and told him, "*In the Batista days, people like you weren't allowed to swim in the beaches.*"

The brave man replied, "*I didn't come back to Cuba so that I could swim in the beach.*"

Another captured invader, a former farmer, asked Castro why there was no democracy in Cuba. Castro, the absolute dictator of the country, replied, "*Who told you that?*"

I desperately hoped to hear about Tío Alberto's whereabouts; I just wanted to know if he was alive. I finally saw a picture in the *Miami Herald* of Tío Alberto facing his captors with his arms tied behind his back. I knew that things would not go well for him; the Cuban leadership knew who he was because he had helped them before in Narcisa.

Castro's guards tortured Tío Alberto in prison for what they called his treason to the revolution. He didn't speak much of those days. Miguel Uría, a family friend who served time with him there, told me that the only place in the prison with sunlight was where they disposed human feces. They named it the "shit patio." Tío Alberto loved the beaches and worshipped the sun— he must have suffered terribly in the dark dungeon where Castro put him.

Seeing Tío Alberto's picture was a relief. Because of his charismatic presence, newspapers always took photographs wherever he went; I guess this special quality was what caused the *Miami Herald* photographer to snap his picture. I was happy to see that he was still alive, although he was clearly in a weakened state.

Tío Alberto's father—my grandfather—participated in the negotiations that led to the prisoners' release. On the day before Christmas in 1962, after the prisoners were freed in exchange for bulldozers and medicine, I saw Tío Alberto again at my grandfather's home in Fort Lauderdale. He was very thin and pale (he'd always sported a magnificent tan) and had a large cyst on his forehead. Tío Alberto was overjoyed to see his wife, Paulette, and his two children, Chico and Potica.

A few days later, President Kennedy appeared at the Orange Bowl and swore that the Brigada 2506 flag would soon fly in a free Havana—another empty promise. Kennedy suggested that General Eisenhower had responsibility for the fiasco since it was his original plan. Eisenhower was a five-star general who had planned and commanded the D-Day invasion. He never would have bungled the operation so severely, nor would he have hesitated to support the invasion force. Kennedy's betrayal is deeply engrained in the minds of Americans of Cuban heritage. I can only hope that one day his empty promise becomes a reality.

THE MISSILE CRISIS: CASTRO ALWAYS WINS

MY FIGHT WITH FIDEL CASTRO IS PERSONAL. AND I HAVE TO admit that, so far, he has won every battle. The U.S. government has challenged him time and again, but Castro always manages to avoid defeat. He is more experienced, devious, and ruthless than the U.S. political establishment. His only goal is to maintain control of his country at all costs; the entire island of Cuba can starve, for all he cares. I feel like I've been fighting a 53-round boxing match—spending much of it face-down on the ground. But sooner or later, I know that Fidel will lick the canvas.

The thirteen days called the Cuban Missile Crisis—or the October Crisis, as it is known in Cuba—have often been portrayed as a victory for John F. Kennedy. After JFK failed to kill Castro with his exploding cigars, Nikita Khrushchev, Premier of the Soviet Union, started building missile bases in Cuba. The Soviets installed medium- and intermediate-range ballistic nuclear missiles that were capable of striking most of the continental United States.

When confronted with the evidence, JFK had no alternative but to act. However, instead of attacking Cuba and removing Castro, he timidly decided to surround the island with ships. JFK called it a "quarantine," but Castro called it what it was—a blockade. Kennedy demanded that the Soviets dismantle the missile bases and remove all of their offensive weapons. In turn, Castro pressured Khrushchev to deploy the nuclear missiles against the people of the United States. He wanted to kill Americans.

Ultimately, Kennedy and Khrushchev made a deal. The Soviets would dismantle their weapons and remove them from Cuba, "*subject to United Nations verification.*" (We all know how trustworthy the U.N. can be.) In exchange, Kennedy was forced to make a public declaration that he would never try to invade again. He gave away my Cuba.

The administration, the media, even Hollywood declared the settlement a big victory for the United States. I beg to differ. How could simply removing the missiles be considered a victory? It was a betrayal of the Cuban and American people. A dire enemy of our nation was allowed to rule over a country only ninety miles from Key West. Castro was never given a reason to truly fear the United States.

I wonder whether Castro still has nuclear missiles; maybe that is what has deterred the United States from acting for so long. After all, Cuba is a large volcanic country with many caverns and mountainous regions. After Tío Alberto became a CIA operative, he showed me pictures of nuclear missiles in Cuba after they were supposedly removed. I saw the photographs.

At the time of the missile crisis, I was eleven years old and attending Bayview Elementary in Fort Lauderdale. Our teachers made us practice hiding under our desks. They couldn't possibly have expected those drills to protect us from a nuclear strike, but we did them every day. I watched U.S. military convoys drive past Oakland Avenue on their way south to the Keys. I was glued to the news, passionately hoping that the end of Castro was near. I prayed hard that we would not be attacked and was relieved that the world did not enter into a nuclear war, as Khrushchev had threatened. Castro would have deployed his missiles against our country if he had had his way.

While I was ducking under my desk at Bayview Elementary, Tío Alberto was enjoying Castro's hospitality as a Bay of Pigs invader. Tío Alberto recalled that every time the U.S.–Cuba conflict escalated, he and the other prisoners were told that they would be executed. During the missile crisis, the death threats became more than just words. Russian tanks were even brought in to surround the prison building.

The warden, William Gálvez, assured Tío Alberto that if the U.S. invaded Cuba, not a single one of the prisoners would survive. One attorney later said that Tío Alberto's prison was "like Devil's Island." The round, stone prison building dated back to the days of Spanish rule. Tío Alberto and 212 of his companions were crammed into one large cell in an abandoned part of the building. Each was assigned a tiny measure of floor space to avoid fights. They lived like that for a year.

In the *Palm Beach Daily News* Tío Alberto sardonically described his prison as "unfurnished." But Tío Alberto always found humor in his misery. As he once said, *"There was one toilet and two showers for all of us."*

Tío Alberto suffered from a bout of dysentery, but his captors refused to give him any medication. After losing sixty-five pounds in three months, he collapsed into a coma and was unconscious for two days. Medication suddenly became available once Castro learned that he would lose a prisoner worth $100,000 (the expected exchange rate). The Missile Crisis was certainly no victory for Tío Alberto or the other prisoners.

CASTRO'S SECRETS REVEALED: THE DICTATOR AND LEE HARVEY OSWALD

PRESIDENT JOHN F. KENNEDY TRIED TO ASSASSINATE THE Cuban dictator, but Castro's agent in America, Lee Harvey Oswald, killed him before he could finish the job. Exploding cigars—please. The Warren Commission investigation was a canard. I know many of you are probably uncomfortable with this theory, but much recent evidence reveals that it's more likely true than not.

Lee Harvey Oswald had many ties to Castro's Cuba. Oswald was trained in the Soviet Union and got into a fight with anti-Castro Cuban exiles here in New Orleans. He was at the Cuban embassy in Mexico shortly before he assassinated Kennedy in Dallas. His own assassin, Jack Ruby, had ties to Cuban mafia, which was closely allied with Castro.

Brian Latell's latest book, *Castro's Secrets*,[11] reveals that Cuban intelligence was aware of the plot to assassinate Kennedy. A Cuban intelligence defector, Florentino Aspillaga, told Latell that his job was to intercept CIA transmissions to U.S. spies in Cuba. However, on the day of the assassination, he was ordered to turn his attention away from Miami and towards Texas. Aspillaga said that Castro knew Kennedy was about to be killed.

If you still doubt that Fidel Castro was involved with

---

[11] Brian Latell, *Castro's Secrets* (Paul Grave MacMillan 2012).

Oswald's plan to assassinate John Kennedy, all you have to do is review the Warren Commission report.[12] The 800-page report shows that our government was unable to understand what happened. Either they were negligent investigators or they intentionally hid evidence to avoid starting a third world war.

According to the Warren Commission report, Oswald's wife, Marina Oswald, testified that sometime in August her husband first told her of his plan to go to Mexico and from there to Cuba, where he planned to stay: "He had given up the plan to hijack an airplane and fly directly to Cuba, which plan Marina consistently opposed. On September 17, 1963, he obtained from the Mexican Consulate General in New Orleans a tourist card."

Oswald took with him a Spanish-English dictionary, his correspondence with the Soviet Embassy in Washington, newspaper clippings concerning his arrest and his interest in the Fair Play for Cuba Committee (Marina testified that Lee Harvey thought the materials would help him once he got to Cuba.) He also brought evidence that he was a director of the New Orleans Chapter of the Committee; notes of his stay in the Soviet Union; and proof of his early interest in communist literature, his ability to speak Russian, and his experience in street agitation.

Ultimately, Oswald made his way to Mexico, where he visited the Cuban Embassy on September 27, 1963—a little less than a month before the assassination. There he met with Mrs. Sylvia Tirado de Duran, a Mexican citizen employed there. According to Mrs. Duran, he wanted to be recognized and accepted as a friend of the Cuban revolution. Oswald then went to the Soviet Embassy and spoke with consulate officials who also served as agents of the KGB.

Oswald returned to the Cuban Embassy, hoping to arrange his trip to Cuba and thereafter to the Soviet Union. He entered

---

[12]The Warren Commission Report, The President's Commission on the Assassination of President Kennedy Delivered by Executive Order No. 11130 on September 24, 1964.

into a discussion there with the Cuban Consul, Eusebio Azque. According to the Warren Commission, "A discussion between Oswald and Azque developed into a heated argument, which ended when Azque told Oswald that in his opinion people like him were harming the Cuban revolution and that so far as Azque was concerned, he would not give Oswald a visa." Mrs. Duran forwarded the Cuban visa application to Havana.

Ultimately, Oswald did not get the Cuban visa. This merits some analysis. If Oswald was a pro-Castro activist in the United States, why would the Cuban government deny him a visa? One real possibility is that Castro did not want any further evidence of Oswald's ties to him. If Oswald went to New Orleans, Castro could communicate with him freely through his agents and still maintain full deniability. If Oswald visited Cuba before assassinating John Kennedy, the connection would become obvious. We now know from Aspillaga's testimony that Castro was well aware that one of his sympathizers was about to kill John Kennedy.

After Jack Ruby killed Oswald, the Warren Commission subjected him to an intense and somewhat mindless investigation. Ruby was given a lengthy polygraph examination where he was asked a number of open-ended questions. Ruby claimed that he did not know Oswald before November 22, 1963, and did not assist him in the assassination. He denied being a member of the Communist Party or doing any business with Castro or Cuba. He claimed that a prior trip to Cuba he made in 1959 was solely for pleasure. He denied that he shot Oswald because of any underworld, foreign, or labor union influence. Then Ruby was asked a surprising question:

Q. "Did you shoot Oswald in order to save Mrs. Kennedy the ordeal of a trial?"

A. "Yes."

Ruby killed Oswald to save Jackie Kennedy the ordeal of a

murder trial? This illogical, obvious lie clearly wasn't the real motivation. However, it was good enough for the Warren Commission, which stopped investigating Ruby's ties to Castro right there.

To me, the most compelling proof is that Castro was aware of Kennedy's plot to assassinate him. Castro would have had no hesitation whatsoever in retaliating against a man who was trying to kill him. None. He has murdered countless people for simply posing a threat. For a man who demanded that the Soviets deploy their nuclear missiles against the United States, killing Kennedy wouldn't have been a big deal. Although Latell doesn't reach this conclusion, I believe that Castro masterminded Kennedy's assassination.

I remember when President Kennedy was assassinated. I was walking the corridors of San Ignacio Jesuit School in Puerto Rico when I heard the news. Obviously, during this time Castro was always on my mind and I assumed, without proof, that he must have had something to do with it. Although I felt that President Kennedy had let my uncle and the invaders down, he did not merit an assassination. I remember feeling powerless and that once again Castro had come out victorious. There was no talk of any substance linking Fidel Castro to the assassination. It was my view then, and it is now, that the United States did not want to be pushed into a third world war and thus the Warren Commission was a cover-up to hide Castro's culpability. Today, I don't feel any different.

HARD WORK AND HARD KNOCKS: LIFE IN PUERTO RICO

My MOTHER REMARRIED EMILIO COSCULLUELA, A DEVELOPER who moved my mother, sisters and me to San Juan, Puerto Rico. He developed a well-known residential section in San Juan called Torrimar. Their marriage led to two children, my brothers Alex and Victor Cosculluela. Thirteen years my junior, Alex works as a lawyer in Houston, while Victor is a professor of philosophy in Florida.

Our family moved with Emilio to Puerto Rico, where I spent my teenage years. After the eighth grade, I entered San Ignacio de Loyola, a Jesuit high school in San Juan. It was a formidable school that was very hard to get into. Classes were taught in both Spanish and English, but you were also expected to speak French. I was highly motivated by the Jesuit seminarians there, particularly one named Father Charles Beirne, S.J., who later taught at Harvard. Students who failed to participate in his class were called "vegetables"; Father Beirne would "plant" them outside our classroom until they had learned their lesson. Beirne expected excellence, much like my mother. Beirne got it.

Because I had to work during my high school years, I couldn't play many sports. However, I played chess with Emilio, who had attained grandmaster level. I soon became one of the best young chess players of Puerto Rico. My children tease me suggesting I was a geek. Perhaps, but playing chess taught me how to stay on the offense and anticipate my opponents' moves. These principles proved to be quite helpful for my legal career.

Our team qualified for Puerto Rico's high school chess championship in San Ignacio. We were matched against a formidable team that had the chess master Julio Kaplan, who was then one of the best young players in the world. There was lot of talk about the match in the months preceding the tournament. I knew that there was no way I could beat Kaplan, but I wanted our team to win the tournament. In order to prevail, I had to think outside the box.

Although I normally sat as first chair for my four-man team, I took the second chair and matched our worst player against Kaplan. This strategy assured that our second, third, and fourth boards would win. Although Kaplan won all four of his games, my team won six points—and the victory for our school. Furious, Kaplan called me a coward, but I didn't care. I knew that team victory was more important.

When I was fifteen, I got a job at a construction site in Torrimar for one of Emilio's companies. No one knew I was Emilio's stepson. He made sure of that. The work, though hard and dirty, made me stronger and more confident; it taught me how to deal with humanity. As a big white kid, I stood out like a sore thumb in a workforce of over 800 Puerto Ricans. It was a rough and intimidating group. We all made $56 a week. I was pretty green and clumsy, and I frequently managed to cut myself on my tools. There was always plenty of blood in whatever ditch I was digging.

One guy in the crew, Luis, obviously didn't like me. Whenever the foreman came by our worksite, Luis would grab my shovel and say, "*Cano* (Blondy), let me show you how it's done." The foreman would catch me standing there like an idiot and admonish me. Then Luis would throw my shovel back once the foreman left. This happened twice. On the third time, I held onto my shovel and called him a *cabrón*. In Cuba, *cabrón* means nothing other than "You are a jerk," but in Puerto Rico it means that your wife runs around on you and you don't care. I didn't know the finer points of Puerto Rican Spanish at that point, but I was about to learn. Luis pulled a curva, a curved knife, from his back pocket and came at me.

Luckily, I had made good friends with a big, muscular black man named Mingo. Mingo dressed sharply and always sported beautiful zirconium rings. We would go to a little restaurant where they fed the workers, and the two girls who worked there always paid particular attention to us and gave us bigger portions. I think Mingo had plans for these girls, but I knew better than to get involved. They were the daughters of the restaurant owner, an intimidating older man who liked to carry around a hatchet in his hand.

Whatever the case, Mingo grabbed a pickaxe and told Luis, "If you cut *el cano*, I will put this through your head." This was no idle boast. A few days earlier, I had seen a worker there chop off three of another man's fingers with a machete. These were violent men. In any event, Luis decided he would not cut me. I made sure to hang around with Mingo a lot after that.

A year later, at another construction site, there was a crane operator who always ridiculed me during the breaks. He was a tall, dark skinny but muscular guy about forty years old. Mingo wasn't in this crew, so when the crane operator's threats got serious, I became pretty worried about the situation. I asked my mother and Emilio for advice.

When I was bullied as a skinny little boy in Cuba, my mother didn't take me to a psychiatrist or report it to the principal. She put pins through the tip of my tennis shoes (three in each shoe) and told me that the next time I got bullied, I should stick them. That stopped the bullying.

This time, to deal with the crane operator, she gave me a pocketknife. She told me to sharpen the knife during the breaks—but never to use it. I was hoping for another less risky solution, but that was what I was told to do. So, during the breaks, I just sharpened that knife and said nothing. The word got around camp that *el cano* was going to cut the crane operator. When asked if I was going to do it, I would not answer. Two days later, the crane operator approached me and quietly whispered that he had just been kidding and didn't want any trouble.

I don't think I would have ever worked pick and shovel in Cuba, but I'm glad I had to as an exile boy. My stories are not unusual for the Cuban exile community. We were forced to become resilient and adapt—lessons that served me well later in life.

"Villa Kibu," the Fowler home

The Fowlers at Villa Kibu, Havana *circa* 1930
My Father is wearing the boots

South terrace

Painting of Royal Arms of Britain used by my Great Great Grandfather during his time in office as the Consul of Britain in Cuba

Ball Room: upstairs location of painting collection

This house belonged to my Great-Granduncle, Alberto Fowler. The Castro government converted it into the Cohiba Cigar Factory. The Cohiba brand was created especially for Fidel Castro

My dad and his brothers and sisters
Back row: Tio Alberto, my Father George Fowler
Front row: Lisette, Carlotta, and Nunu Fowler

The Fowler Outlaws
Juan Weiss, Mother, Fort Pipes, Paulette Fowler, Sam Giberga

Narcisa II, Yacht stolen from us by Castro in October 1960

My Father, George Fowler

George Fowler,
Consul of Britain,
my Great Great
Grandfather

George Fowler,
My Grandfather

George Fowler
(Father) at 2¹/₂ and Duke

Me

George Fowler, IV (my Son) and
George Fowler V (my Grandson)

General Arsene Perrilliat of New Orleans, my paternal Great Grandfather

Me as Roy Rogers with my father, mother, sisters Lita and Lisette. This was taken before Castro in Varadero Beach right before we left Cuba in May, 1960

Me pictured seated in the center, dressed in white. La Salle School

Picture of my present family: Cristi Fowler Chauvin, Christian Chauvin, holding my Grandson Christian Chauvin, Jennifer Walker Fowler, holding my Grandson George Fowler V, George Fowler IV, Cristina and me

Mother and Father

My Mother and Father's
wedding

My Mother and Father's
wedding

My Mother and
Father's wedding
Pictured far left:
Nene Aguilera, my
maternal
Grandmother.
Pictured second from
right: Santiago
Estevez, my maternal
Grandfather.

My maternal Great
Grandfather Julian Aguilera

My maternal Great
Grandmother "Mamicota,"
Matilde Aguilera

FACHADA PRINCIPAL

LAS GRANDES MANSIONES HABANERAS

VILLA VIEJO

SECCIÓN A CARGO DE RENÉE DE GARCÍA KHOLY

Sra. MATILDE DE CUADRA DE AGUILERA.

Kasanjian.

57

ENTRE las más bellas construcciones que rodean el pintoresco estanque del Country Club Park se destaca "Villa Viejo", residencia de los estimados esposos Matilde de Cuadra y Julián Aguilera, en la que habitan también el joven matrimonio Nena Aguilera y Santiago Estévez, con su hijita Matilde Graciella.

Llama la atención por sus líneas del más puro estilo español del Norte, cubiertas todas por espesa yedra.

El alero, sostenido por vigas de madera tallada, está cubierto en su interior por brillante losa sevillana, que le da una nota viva y alegre con sus variados colores.

Hermosos jardines, aterciopelados lawns, fuentes y adornos típicos completan el delicioso conjunto.

En medio del parque se levanta un precioso arco de porcelana de Talavera, entre dos bancos del mismo material al que una afiligranada reja de hierro forjado sirve de respaldo.

Villa Viejo. Fidel Castro uses this home

ENTRADA

den admirarse las magníficas cenefas de mosaicos sevillanos, con reflejos metálicos que adornan la escalera.

Esta es de losetas rojas, que armonizan con las anchas vigas de madera tallada.

Al frente se ostenta un gran escudo también en esos famosos mosaicos. A la derecha una curiosa pila de agua bendita, de loza antigua, que procede de la fundación del Convento de Santa Teresa, según documento que acredita su autenticidad.

La valiosa colección de armas que posee el señor Aguilera, empieza a admirarse desde la entrada, donde se ven ejemplares de indiscutible mérito.

COMEDOR.

Delante, un hermoso estanque bordeado también de losetas de Talavera, con cuatro grandes ranas en las esquinas, rodeado de fragantes flores.

Entre un bello macizo luce un típico tinajón de Camagüey, sostenido por cuatro pies de hierro, en el que se lee la evocadora fecha de 1830.

Más allá, entre las más raras especies de dalias y gladiolos, está el gran court de tennis, que completa el espléndido parque.

Penetremos en el interior.

Es indudable que para decorar una casa en estilo obligado hay que tener gran conocimiento de él y muy buen gusto.

Este es el caso de esta residencia, en la que el señor Aguilera, "connaisseur" y aficionado entusiasta del estilo español antiguo, ha sabido reunir y combinar con tacto exquisito todos los detalles de su elegante casa.

Desde la entrada pue-

En el Vestíbulo del primer piso, una hermosísima armadura recuerda épocas de hazañas y conquistas. En la pared un cuadro de mosaicos al frente, y al lado opuesto, un magnífico óleo, por cierto, de histórico linaje.

El barandaje de madera de columnas torneadas es de un labrado maravilloso.

Al pie de ella un gran reloj con ricos bronces, que firma Herraiz de Madrid, de donde son

VISTA GENERAL DEL PARQUE.

también la mayor parte de los muebles de la casa.

Un hermoso San Francisco, el "poverello", llena uno de los testeros.

Lindos jarrones de Talavera y faroles cincelados terminan felizmente el decorado del vestíbulo.

El Salón principal es muy elegante y confortable.

Sobre las finas losas españolas del piso luce una rica alfombra, de la Real Fábrica de Madrid, con los más exquisitos dibujos y colores.

Los techos son de vigas de madera esculpida artísticamente.

Sus paredes están decoradas en color beige suave, que hacen resaltar los anchos marcos de madera que rodean las puertas y ventanas, adornadas con grandes cortinajes de damasco color cereza.

En la mesa del centro se admira un vaso de cerámica, bibelots, libros antiguos, etc.

Un bargueño con ricos bronces, un magnífico arcón y banco sofá, de forma típica, cubiertos de

PORTAL TERRAZA.

FUENTE DEL COMEDOR.

ASPECTO DEL GRAN SALON.

damasco, adornan los distintos testeros.

Un hermoso canapé forrado de cuero de Córdoba, entre grandes poltronas, forma el estrado.

Sillas de cuero policromado, fraileros y butacas, completan el mueblaje. La lámpara de pie, de madera tallada, llena uno de los huecos junto al sofá.

En las paredes lucen valiosos óleos, destacándose entre ellos uno que representa una bailarina española.

A un extremo del salón un antiquísimo brasero de cobre y madera tallada. Dos vitrinas llenas de abanicos y joyas de familia de gran valor, llenan los testeros principales.

El comedor es una pieza hermosísima.

El piso de alegres losetas armoniza con el reflejo de las preciosas cenefas sevillanas.

El techo de grandes vigas es de un esmerado labrado artístico.

Los severos y elegantes muebles son una obra exquisita que hace honor a

los industriales y obreros cubanos.

Un precioso repostero de damasco, con gran escudo de armas, adorna el panel principal.

Frente a éste, el hermoso buffet, sobre el que lucirán candelabros, pájaros de plata y una inmensa sopera cincelada con corona de rico metal, que perteneció a una de las más linajudas y aristocráticas familias cubanas.

NENA AGUILERA DE ESTE-VEZ y su hija MATILDE GRACIELLA. Encanto.

Llama la atención un plato cincelado que es el clou de los adornos del comedor; una obra maravillosa del Padre Granda, el famoso artista madrileño, cuyos trabajos son tan admirados y solicitados. Un paravent de damasco rojo con soportes de hierro forjado, muy elegante, cierra la entrada.

En el extremo opuesto del comedor una linda fuente de Talavera, con sus juegos de agua, alegra y refresca el recinto.

En curiosos estantes esquineros se admira una vajilla de porcelana sevillana legítima de Triana.

A la salida del comedor, una agradable terraza, o comedor de verano, adornada de finos muebles de mimbre, sirve de expansión y recreo. Una estatua de Venus Ac... es el pal adorno, entre un grupo de hermosas palm...s.

Jaulas con pájaros y una gran pecera, dan un aspecto de dulce placidez al recinto.

Le sigue un saloncito de música, coqueto y confortable, para las veladas de invierno.

Al lado opuesto de la casa se encuentra la gran terraza principal. Sus hermosas dimensiones, preciosos pisos y cenefas y sus arcos cubiertos de yedra le dan un aspecto fantástico.

Mimbres, jarrones y plantas la adornan.

La vista ideal de los jardines del poético lago, el mar, a lo lejos y el ambiente delicioso de paz ...

TINAJON DE CAMAGÜEY.

60

Alicia Foyo de Aguilera,
"Manina," my Godmother,
a champion golfer at the Biltmore

BACK TO AMERICA: MEETING CRISTINA AND HER FAMILY

AT SEVENTEEN, AFTER I GRADUATED FROM JESUIT HIGH SCHOOL in 1968, I moved to Baton Rouge to study business at Louisiana State University. My immediate family stayed in Puerto Rico then moved to Miami that same year. Back in the pre-Castro days, if your family had an interest in sugar, you would send your children to the LSU Agricultural College. There you would study agriculture before returning to manage the sugar plantations at home. My father had gone to LSU—although recently an old friend of his told me that he had never formally registered.

At the time, LSU was mostly a party and football school. I found the curriculum fairly boring after San Ignacio, and a good portion of the student body wasn't interested in an education. It wasn't the right place for me, but I am a Tiger fan.

At LSU, nobody much cared about Cuba or Castro. Student demonstrations were usually only about Vietnam. Much of our country—much of the world, in fact—believed that Castro was a swell guy who freed the people of Cuba. Reporters swooned over the dictator, and Che was widely romanticized by professors and students. The students wear t-shirts with his face on them.

On campus, I frequently spoke out against Fidel Castro and protested the regime. A girl named Cristina Jenkins soon approached me and said that she admired my speeches. She asked me to help her carry out a demonstration against *Life* magazine, which had named Fidel Castro "Man Of The Year." I guess he must have won the award for killing more people than anybody else that year. We set fire to the magazines and chanted. Although our protest didn't attract much attention, it was worth it. It gave me a chance to get to know Cristina—and, ultimately, to marry her. It's corny to say, but it was love at first sight. For forty-one years I have been married to a woman that is totally aligned with me on values, yet 180° opposite me in personality. I am Germanic, efficient and organized. She is lovely.

Cristina and I were married on December 19, 1971, at the LSU chapel. Today, we have two children, both married, and two grandsons. My children married well. My son, George Fowler IV, married a wonderful woman, Jennifer Walker; their child, George Fowler V, was born on the 4th of July in 2011. We call him Quintus. My daughter, Cristina Fowler, married Christian Chauvin. Christian is a successful insurance man and was the starting kicker for LSU and Tennessee. Their son, Christian Chauvin Jr., was born on May 22, 2011. We call him Dudie. I am blessed to have such a wonderful family, and I hope to get more grandchildren. I know another one is on the way, Jack. My family is my greatest joy in life. I hang with Quintus and Dudie and soon with Jack.

Both of my children went to undergraduate and law school at Tulane and passed the bar. They both live blocks from my house. George IV now works as a developer; I am a frequent investor in his business, Fowler Development. I talk to George several times a day. He is a man of character and integrity. My daughter Cristi is a lawyer with my firm and takes charge of the firm's marketing efforts in all its offices. I call her Cristi "The Locomotive." She is beautiful and sweet, but always gets what she wants. I have never won an argument with her. We are a close knit family.

Both of my wife's parents, Eduardo and Mercedita Jenkins, came from Varadero Beach. As Cuban refugees, they settled in Baton Rouge.

You might think that "Eduardo Jenkins" is an odd last name for a Cuban. He was supposedly the direct descendant of Admiral Robert Jenkins, a British captain. The Spaniards called him a pirate and cut his ear off in Cuba. It was recorded as the "War of Jenkins' Ear."[13] Although Eduardo preferred to think of his ancestor as an admiral, it's clear to me that he had inherited pirate blood.

Eduardo was a magnificent athlete in Cuba, where he rowed on a crew, swam, and even coached for his local club. Since he was always heavily suntanned, he was known as *"El Negro"* Jenkins. His father worked in the sugar business and had built up a sizeable estate, but his mother died young after suffering from paralysis. He was brought up primarily by two nannies who doted on him hand and foot.

Mercedita was the most endearing human being you could ever meet—soft-spoken, smart, well-read, and utterly charismatic. Like my wife, she was the kind of person who made whoever she was talking to feel very special. Self-deprecating and self-effacing, she knew how to flatter her guests. No matter what stupid thing you might say, she would act like it was a magnificent revelation or discovery. She was a fine contrast to Eduardo, who was gruff, to the point, and stern. However, like my wife, Mercedita usually got her way.

Mercedita was the daughter of Don Pedro Alcebo, one of the wealthiest men in Varadero Beach. Alcebo's large home was close to the Batista residence. In her early years, Mercedita was exceptionally beautiful and charming—she was crowned the Queen of Varadero Beach.

---

[13]The War of Jenkins' Ear was between England and Spain from 1739 to 1748.

Her marriage to the athletic, popular Eduardo Jenkins was inevitable. The event was celebrated with much pomp and circumstance as they walked under the oars of Eduardo's fellow crewmembers. Like my parents, the Jenkins were spoiled children. Men like Eduardo partied hard; because they were the elite, they felt entitled to all of life's pleasures—and pre-Castro Cuba afforded many pleasures. He was a man of character and a hard worker devoted to his family.

Notwithstanding, their life in Cuba was unique. Eduardo ran both his own plantations and those that Mercedita had inherited from her father. He was a gifted rancher and planter; his ranches and plantations were immaculately kept and provided the family with a sizeable income.

Then came Fidel. Eduardo quickly realized that Fidel was no friend of his, and he and his friends in Varadero plotted to overthrow the new regime. They had no sympathy for the *revolución*, and Fidel knew it.

Fidel moved swiftly to eliminate any possibility of insurrection. Before and during the invasion, Fidel arrested anyone who could remotely cause problems for his thriving revolution. One of those people was Eduardo. Along with many of his friends and relatives, he was captured and incarcerated in San Severino Prison.

In the aftermath of the Bay of Pigs, Eduardo was asked to step into the center of the fort, under the gaze of the guards in the tower. Now that he was the center of attention, his fellow prisoners also watched from their cells around him. Fidel Castro himself emerged and looked down from one of the towers. Castro asked, "*So, you are Eduardo Jenkins?*"

Eduardo looked up and said, "Yes, I am Eduardo Jenkins."

Castro again asked, "So, you are Eduardo Jenkins?"

Eduardo said, "I already told you, I am Eduardo Jenkins."

Schooled in Marxist interrogation techniques of that era,

Castro asked him yet again, *"So—you are Eduardo Jenkins?"*

To which Mr. Jenkins replied not at all.

Castro asked the question again, and Eduardo again did not reply. Then Castro asked, *"So, you are the brother of the traitor?"*

At this point, Eduardo was puzzled. His brother, Gaston, was a prominent doctor in Varadero who had been caught assisting the counterrevolutionary forces. Short, stocky, and tough, Gaston disguised himself as a nun in order to administer medical aid to the anti-Castro rebels. Eventually he was caught and imprisoned along with Eduardo in San Severino Fort.

Gaston was starved and then forced to get down on his hands and knees to eat in front of the other prisoners while the guards sneered at him. They said that he ate like a dog, to which Gaston replied, *"I may eat like a dog now, but you all are the real dogs."*

In the days preceding Eduardo's encounter with Castro, Gaston had been taken outside the prison to *el paredón* on numerous occasions. Each time, the guards told Eduardo that his brother was going to be shot. This last time, Gaston had not been returned to his cell. Eduardo believed that his brother had been assassinated, so he was confused by Castro's question.

Castro said, *"Though the revolution has been generous to your brother, he has betrayed it. He has escaped and exiled himself in an embassy, and he seeks to leave the country."* Castro vowed that he would never let Gaston leave Cuba without receiving just punishment. *"So therefore, you are the brother of a traitor,"* he told Eduardo.

Eduardo said, *"I don't think I'm the brother of a traitor; rather, I'm the brother of a very smart man."* His fellow prisoners broke out in a chorus of laughter—not just from amusement, but from their pride in this man who had the courage to talk back to the feared dictator. Eduardo thought he certainly would be shot, but he got away with it.

Gaston's cellmates nicknamed him *"El Cojonauta"*—from the

word for "astronaut" in Spanish ("astronauta") and from "cojones," or "balls." Castro was so furious because Gaston had tricked him into believing he had become a supporter of the *revolución*. Castro even allowed him to work as a doctor at one of the hospitals. Gaston asked if his wife could leave Cuba for the U.S. to pick up their three daughters. Shortly after she left the country, the jeep that transported Gaston to the hospital was found overturned—and the three thugs who guarded him were found dead. *El Cojonauta* was not a man to be messed with.

Mercedita was devastated by the *revolución*, but she sought to help Eduardo any way she could. She was a frequent visitor to the prison and tried to give him whatever comforts the prison guards would allow her. She, too, was subject to great abuse and ridicule. A captain there asked her for sexual favors in exchange for better treatment for her husband. She rebuffed that pig.

Many of the Cubans who came to power were scum who exploited their newly found authority over their prior bosses. The more pain they inflicted on the helpless members of the opposition and the former upper class, the more favor they would gain with their leaders. Notwithstanding, there were many good people in Cuba who tried to help Mercedita and Eduardo.

In the midst of this confusing and distressful situation, Mercedita heard that Castro planned to send the youth of Cuba to Russia to be trained in Soviet Marxism. Greatly frightened, she made arrangements with CIA operatives to obtain false passports for her children—Cristina, Mercedes, Vicky, and Carmen—to travel to the United States and escape the threat of deportation to Russia.

On September 5, 1961, Cristina and her three sisters left their mother, their imprisoned father, and their life in beautiful Cuba to become refugees. Upon her arrival in the United States, twelve-year-old Cristina was asked whether she wanted the assistance of Catholic Charities. Not understanding English, once she heard the word "Catholic," she promptly agreed. She and her sisters were then put under the authority of the Catholic Charities Program.

Like many children of anti-Castro Cubans of that era, they were then moved to the U.S. pursuant to a program called the Peter Pan Program. Other former Peter Pan kids include Xavier Suarez, the former Mayor of Miami; Carlos Gutierrez, U.S. Secretary of Commerce; U.S. Senator Mel Martinez; and many other prominent Cuban exiles. Since then, several studies have revealed the harmful pressures and difficulties felt by the children in this program.

Cristina and her sisters were sent to a school in Indiana, where her older brother, Ed, had been sent earlier in the year to study. She kept a daily diary of their trip. Frankly, I can't start reading it without tearing up. It was a terribly trying experience for a twelve-year-old girl, but she faced the trials and tribulations with her characteristic courage and character. Her diary is optimistic and hopeful, not because there was cause to be, but because Cristina had no choice; she was in charge of her three little sisters ad she was going to pull them through. I asked Vicky to write her experience. Here it is verbatim. Castro will pay.

The Jenkins Sisters Escape to America

On September 3, 1961, I remember being told to wake up and made to dress quickly, we were leaving to go on vacation to the U.S.A., as I was constantly reminded for weeks before. We left our beautiful, comfortable home in Varadero for Havana. My mother, the nanny (Eloina) and the family's driver took all four of us to stay at the home of my Uncle Oscar Alcebo, mother's brother, in Havana before leaving for the United States.

All the way to Havana I kept hearing my mother telling us we had to be at our very best behavior, and to mind Cristina who was going to take care of us. Cristina was the oldest, twelve years old. Mercedes was ten, I was six and Carmen was five years old. Off we went to Havana to wait out our turn to leave. My mother seemed very upset and nervous and was waiting apparently for the call she needed to hear before taking us to the airport. Finally, the big day arrived and all four of us left for the airport. Again, Carmen and I were reminded to keep quiet the whole time. I remember we were allowed to take our favorite porcelain dolls with us on the trip.

I didn't know what to think at my age, I had never been to an airport, and thinking back, I never in my life saw so many people in one place, running, children crying for their parents not to leave them etc., I kept wondering why would children be crying if they were going on a vacation like us to have fun? Anyway, many strange thoughts occurred to me that day, but I remember Cristina taking charge, reminding us not to talk or ask questions, or we would be told to stay and not go on the vacation. So the whole time all of us girls kept very quiet. No sooner than we got to the airport, we were taken to a room and told to undress. I will never forget how scared I was looking at the woman dressed in faded green olive fatigues with a big rifle hanging from her shoulder. All around the place I kept seeing all these men and women dressed the same holding guns. The first thing they did was to ask us to leave any valuables. Cristina and Mercedes had to take off their earrings and leave them with the woman. However, she forgot to take Carmen's and mine off.

After this, we were told to go to another room to wait

for our flight. We did just that and Cristina made us sit quickly and kept telling us to keep quiet. (Wow, I have never been so quiet in my life, but I did what was told and kept quiet.) I remember watching my mother and the nanny from the other side. We were separated by a big glass window. I was wondering why she was crying, after all, I would see her soon. I remember some children crying really hard after being told to sit while watching their parents on the other side of the glass window. Those children were pulled out and told to go back to their parents that they were not going to travel that day. The parents begged the guards to allow them to go that they just needed their help to calm down. The guard kept pushing them out and refused hearing more pleas from the parents. Cristina reminded us that that could happen to us if we dared to talk. So, we sat there quietly, watching our mother cry, on the other side of the glass window until we were finally called to board the plane on September 5, 1961.

While boarding the plane, Cristina had to give the guards the passports one more time, and one of the guards asked Carmen and I to hand over our earrings and asked for the dolls, too. The guard broke our dolls' arms and legs, and kept looking inside the body cavities as if he was searching for something. Carmen was already getting agitated and began to cry when Cristina took Carmen's hand and calmed her down and told her not to worry, that she was going to fix the dolls when we got to the states. The guards finally allowed us to board the plane with other children. Cristina told Carmen and me that the guards were looking for money and that's why they broke our dolls' legs.

Finally, the plane took off for Miami, and I will never

forget how quiet everyone was the whole way. Believe me; you could hear a pin drop. What an impression it left on me! That day seemed very long and when we got to Miami airport, Cristina took all of us and sat us away, where nobody could hear, to tell us what she was prepared to say after we landed. I never forget how sad she was, almost crying, telling us that now she could tell us the truth. That the reason for us coming to the United States was that Castro was taking children to Russia, and I remember Carmen asking Cristina what's Russia? Cristina said a very bad place for children and that it was communist country. Carmen asked her later what that word meant. Cristina tried her best to explain and reminded us again to not ask too many questions, either. As for me, I was confused and started to think that there was not going to be any vacation after all. It was starting to hit me a little; I was already feeling tired, very drained and sad from the whole day's experience. I realized that maybe I would never see my parents again, that my father would be killed by Castro. That I would not see my home, Varadero or my dog Kim, a mixed breed, either. I kept silent because I did not want to upset my sister Cristina, who was already very sad and stressed from the heavy burden placed on her shoulders. She was now our mother!

In Miami, we were taken by the Catholic Charities along with other children. The rooms were big with lots of bunk beds. All of us that came on the flight were there also. We stayed in Miami for two weeks. Cristina was made to sign some papers, and thinking we were going to go to a private school in Indiana, she signed them, not really understanding what she had signed. We left for St. Vincent, Indiana soon after. The flight for me seemed eternal. However, I did enjoy it when the stewardess offered lots of Chiclets (gum) to us. Carmen had a whole mouthful.

We finally landed in Indiana where again a social worker was waiting to take us to our new home, St. Vincent School in Evansville. Nobody spoke the whole way there, and finally we came upon a very big home, not much illumination on a very cold chilly night. It was so cold; I was impressed by the smoke coming out of my mouth. I made my sisters laugh when I showed them. The place looked very spooky to me, something you see in a movie. It was an old home built around an apple orchard field. The place was in a very desolate town, hardly any homes or stores. When our car pulled up a nun was already waiting for us. She opened the door and we were told to wait, the social worker left and we never saw her again.

This very first night, was my worst nightmare, and one I will never forget. Another nun came to get Carmen and me, when Carmen started crying very loudly, almost bawling telling Cristina not to leave us alone. I started crying also, but followed, as I left my sisters Cristina and Mercedes behind trying to explain in Spanish to the nun not to separate us, on that first night. They said (in Spanish) that it was too soon, we had just left our home, country, and parents behind, that we were too young to understand what just transpired. However, the nun did not consent to this, and we were literally dragged to our dorm. Carmen kept crying and was inconsolable that night. I remember all the other girls sleeping telling us to hush, to keep quiet. I felt miserable because I wanted to tell them that we were not from here, that we were from Cuba and could not speak the language. I wanted so desperately to tell them how I felt but couldn't. That night we were helped by two girls to undress and put our pajamas. Carmen was led to her bed, located in the very back of the dorm, and I was to sleep in the third row close to the front of the room. The nun's quarter was also located in the same room on the side.   Every room had a nun running that particular dorm.   That same night, Carmen was still inconsolable, kept asking me to come and get her, that she was afraid, the room was very dark no lights. Carmen said that she wanted to go back to Cuba, and see our parents.   I was also scared as the room was very big, and you could hear the winter winds howling all through the night. I told Carmen to meet me half way and, I would go halfway and get her and take her back to my bed. We did just that. Suddenly around six o'clock a.m. both Carmen and I were awakened by a nun hitting us with a big wooden paddle. I did not know why. I kept asking the nun in Spanish what we did wrong. I could not understand her nor could she me. Carmen started to cry to the point of screaming. The nun quickly slapped her.   I went crazy now, started yelling for Cristina, screaming and stomping my feet on the ground. The nun called for some of the girls to come and hold me down, while she grabbed Carmen and led her to her bed, turned out the lights and shut the door behind.

This was really frightening to us as we could not communicate in English and ask why? We did not know why we were being punished. However, in the nights to come Carmen and I still slept together, knowing well that we would be awakened by the big brown paddle the following morning and all the other mornings after that. Carmen was so scared, she started wetting the bed. Then the nun would paddle her more for it. I kept trying to explain, even using sign language for the nun to understand, but it was useless. She kept taking Carmen back to her dark bed.

Finally, I was able to tell my sisters at breakfast what had happened and one of my cousins who could speak English spoke to the nuns about the situation. I could tell my sisters and cousin were very upset. My cousin explained that the nun wanted for us to sleep in our own bed, that every girl had their own bed to sleep on. It was unnecessary for us to sleep together. However, my cousin explained to the nun that we were still traumatized from leaving our beloved country and parents behind. The nuns never understood us or cared to. I remember when my brother Ed found out we were staying at this orphanage and planned a trip to see us. He was living with my American Aunt Wilma, and two cousins in Angola, Indiana. My brother Ed saved up all his money from his newspaper route to come and visit us at the orphanage. I never forget seeing him for the first time after he left Cuba in 1960. (At that time Castro was taking all the young boys to be trained militarily in Russia, they were to be part of Castro's military.) My parents quickly sent Eduardo out first from Cuba. My brother came with big bags of sweets for all four of us. The nuns grabbed the bags away saying all of us had to share, but it was not enough to go around for everyone. Carmen and I were left without any sweets at all.

I remember Cristina talking to Eduardito a lot that day, begging him to help take Carmen and me out of the place. It was not a nice place for us to be in. Eduardito finally left us that day, feeling overwhelmed and sad. He tried very hard to get us out; he begged my cousin Tuty and her new husband, Larry, to get us out. I remember after the Christmas holidays we were led to a room when all of a sudden I saw my cousin Tuty for the first time in years. She was so sweet, tears were coming out of her eyes, and she spoke very softly in Spanish telling us that she had come to pick us up and take us to live with her. Carmen and I were fascinated. Finally, we were with someone that was family, and spoke Spanish. That same day we left St. Vincent's Orphanage in Indiana and lived with my cousins in Indianapolis, Indiana until my parents arrived in the United States in 1963, when Kennedy exchanged medicine for political prisoners. My parents came to the United States in the first Red Cross ship.

I still remember the sad look on my sisters' faces, as Cristina and Mercedes were being left behind alone. Again, I was separated from my sisters, but now in the hands of a family member that offered all her love to us. Looking back, I did not know if I would ever see them again as I was too young to comprehend everything that was taking place in my life at the moment. It was all too fast and surreal. For many years I would not talk or think about that part of my life. That left me marked forever. How my life changed so quickly at age six, my comfort, my home, parents, and country, but more so, for my sister Cristina who at her age had to take on another role, that of a young mother!

Cristina and her older sister, Mercedes, went to live with a farming couple and their children in Indiana. The farmers were a poor and uneducated family. They helped the two Jenkins girls not only out of their own kindness, but also because the government would help them financially.

Eduardo was finally released from the prison and asked to

leave the country as a persona non grata. Ultimately, all the Jenkins were reunited in Laurel, Mississippi, where the children went to school and later LSU in Baton Rouge, Louisiana.

Cristina is a true Latin beauty—feminine in every way, soft of heart, and generous. After Hurricane Katrina struck New Orleans, she helped everybody within her reach. I knew better than to raise an eyebrow when she took out the checkbook. But Cristina's true generosity comes from her heart. Like her mother, she treats everybody like they are special. When she speaks to you, you feel that you are the most important person in the world. She is equally kind to both the president of a company and the doorman. She is renowned for being late to everything; it takes her hours to get to a party and hours to leave it.

Cristina has stood by me through the most difficult moments of my life, whether professionally or personally. She has refused to allow me to entertain my fears or worries. She is a Cuban steel magnolia.

I had a very close relationship with Mercedes, my mother-in-law. She always called it the way it was, and I loved her for that. Charming, funny, sweet, and loving, she played the piano like an angel and could play anything. Whenever I was in my cups, I would try to sing with her. She always told me that although I sang very well, it didn't sound too good. I often sang her a funny song in Spanish—in English it goes, *"When my mother-in-law dies / I hope she's buried upside-down / If she tries to get out / She'll go deeper down."*

After Mercedita died, my wife went to retrieve her things. She found boxes full of newspaper clippings of my anti-Castro work. Mercedita was my biggest fan. Like the other women I have written about, she had no tolerance for Castro's injustices.

MY LAW CAREER

AFTER GRADUATING FROM LSU, I WENT TO TULANE University Law School and graduated in 1975. I started my legal career with relish. I always wanted to be a lawyer. I think you are either born to be a trial lawyer or not. My career as a trial lawyer has been a passion. I have never worked a day in my life because I love what I do. My clients are my good friends. I went to work at Phelps Dunbar, a silk stocking, blue blood New Orleans law firm now almost 200 years old. At the time, it was one of the preeminent maritime law firms in the country, rivaled only by Haight Gardner Poor & Havens in New York which no longer exists.

At Phelps, I trained with some of the best maritime lawyers in the world. My ability to speak Spanish was a great asset to the law firm, and I formed the firm's Latin American Department. Later, I headed the firm's international practice.

My aggressive litigation style was effective, and I soon developed a significant book of business. The firm noticed and made me a partner after only four years. Over the years, I obtained a string of successful legal victories against some of the top legal names in the country, dealing with many interesting cases involving maritime disasters. I have traveled all over the world in my practice.

In 1988, I resigned from Phelps Dunbar and started my own firm. This made the front page of the *CityBusiness*, the New Orleans business newspaper, under the headline "Vanishing Loyalties." The article claimed that no one had ever left Phelps Dunbar after making partner. Many people were surprised at my move and predicted our firm's imminent demise. We proved them wrong. This year we will celebrate our twenty-five year anniversary, and I believe we have the maritime law firm with the most experience and depth of knowledge in this field. Of course, that is just my opinion. If a major marine disaster occurs in the Western Hemisphere, you can assume that our firm will be considered to handle it. Our firm, Fowler Rodriguez, has offices in Miami, New Orleans, Houston, Gulfport, Mobile, Bogota and Cartagena, Colombia.

Our client base is outstanding. For example, twenty years ago, Carnival Corporation—which owns fifty percent of the world's cruise industry—began searching for the number one maritime firm in the world to represent them. They looked in London and New York before ending up in New Orleans. We got the work—beating out two other New Orleans law firms on the short list—and have kept it for twenty years.

New Orleans is now the hotbed for legal maritime practice. The city boasts one of the world's largest ports, barge traffic on the Mississippi River, and—even more importantly—the offshore oil industry. We are counsel to BP in the Deepwater Horizon case. The firm represents most of the large offshore oil drillers and supply boat companies, as well as many of the oil companies and their insurers, such as Lloyds of London. I worked as a lawyer against the Obama Administration in the oil moratorium case.

Throughout my career, I worked to help benefit the Cuban and Latin American community in New Orleans. I am particularly proud of having founded the New Orleans Hispanic Heritage Foundation. Now in its twenty-fourth year, the organization puts on an annual black-tie gala event called the Azucar Ball. All the proceeds go to Latin American children in the New Orleans area whose families have a financial need. Children who demonstrate academic excellence are given scholarships to help them go to private schools.

The New Orleans Hispanic Heritage Foundation is now well recognized and respected, and it has given out over 432 scholarships so far. The New Orleans community and other corporations outside of Louisiana lend their support to the organization. Its board is comprised of Latin Americans from many different countries. I was happy to accept the Presidency this year, but the credit goes to my secretary of nearly thirty years, Rosa Rodriguez. She does a significant amount of the work for our volunteer organization and does it with love.

All through the years of my career, I never forgot about Castro or the crimes he has continued to commit against my country. As General Counsel of the Foundation, I have the opportunity to use my legal experience against the dictator in an effort to bring him to justice.

From 1975 after graduation from law school until approximately 1990, I waged my own war against Fidel Castro. I did it through demonstrations, letters to the editor, and any other form of communication to combat the lies that Castro spewed. With the exception of my family and some very loyal Cuban Americans that live here in New Orleans, it was a lonely battle because I was against trade with the dictator. I was accused by some of being "anti-trade." I was devoted to trying to make New Orleans once again the gateway to the Americas, and worked hard in various organizations supporting the City and the State, but my position on Cuba branded me anti-trade. This was not fair.

Then, I joined the Cuban American National Foundation, and I was no longer fighting alone.

JORGE MAS CANOSA AND THE CUBAN AMERICAN NATIONAL FOUNDATION

WE LIKE TO JOKE THAT EVERY CUBAN BELIEVES HIMSELF TO BE an expert on anything. Take Castro, for an extreme example—he confidently uses Cuba like a guinea pig to test out his theories. Predictably, the dictator's ridiculous experiments have often gone terribly wrong.

Castro once read an article that praised the nutritional value of *gandul*, a kind of shrub prized for its beans. Arbitrarily deciding that it would be the ideal food for cattle, Castro ordered *gandul* to be planted throughout the island. Unfortunately, the cows didn't like the plant and refused to eat it. They must have not read the article.

Furious, Fidel blamed the farmers, who were just following orders. The Cuban government refused to contradict the dictator and instead tried to cover up the truth about the cows' tastes. As José Luis Llovio-Menéndez writes in his book *Insider*[14]: "The cows preferred starvation to Fidel's brainstorm." As the cattle grew thinner and thinner, Fidel found someone to blame for the disaster and moved on to his next experiment. After all, El Comandante is never wrong.

This brand of stubbornness is not unique to Castro; it is a character trait shared by many Cubans. I must confess that I

[14]José Luis Llovio-Menéndez, *Insider* (Bantam Books, 1988).

have some of it myself. I have never been good at taking orders and always walked to the beat of my own drum. For two decades, I waged my own personal war on Fidel. It was frustrating to feel like there was no one to turn to for leadership. Finally, I met a man I didn't mind following. His name was Jorge Mas Canosa, and it was hard for me to even follow his lead.

Brilliant, dynamic, and articulate, Jorge Mas Canosa was by all accounts the greatest of the Cuban exile leaders. As founder of the Cuban American National Foundation, he achieved great fame and respect in our community over the course of his life.

Jorge had an uncanny ability to convince people that they were important to him and to the cause. I felt like he had singled me out during the years I worked with him, but after his death I realized that he made everyone feel that way. His enthusiasm and optimism for a free and democratic Cuba was contagious. To Jorge, everything was urgent—Fidel would be removed from power tomorrow, and we were the ones to make it happen.

Jorge refused to tell the media that he was uninterested in being president of Cuba—after all, he was. He took a backseat to no one. If Jorge was going back to Cuba, he was going back as its president. I had no problem with that; I already had witnessed his phenomenal business and management skills. He was successful as the founder of MasTec, a publicly held construction company that was recently rated the largest Hispanic-owned company in the States.

He once told me that I would eventually help him ensure that Cuba's legal system was efficient and corruption-free. Jokingly but seriously, I told him that that legal system could end his presidency. Jorge acted as he saw fit, throwing caution to the wind.

Born in Santiago de Cuba on September 21, 1939, Jorge was always passionate about Cuba. As a student leader at the University of Havana, he fought against the Batista dictatorship and then later against Fidel. After Castro repeatedly arrested him for speaking out against the dictatorship, Jorge exiled himself to Miami and joined the Bay of Pigs invasion force as a member of Brigade 2506. Following the invasion, he graduated as a Second Army Lieutenant at Fort Benning, Georgia.

Jorge established the Cuban American National Foundation in 1981 in order to influence U.S.–Cuba policy and promote democracy and human rights in Cuba. President Ronald Reagan, who was one of Jorge's good friends, inspired him to create the organization.

I first became involved with the Foundation in the early 1990s when I arranged for two of its most prominent leaders, Francisco "Pepe" Hernández and Domingo Moreira, to speak at Antoine's Restaurant in New Orleans. A good friend of mine from New Orleans, Mike Graugnard, joked that while the Bolsheviks started their revolution in the streets of Moscow, I started ours at Antoine's feasting on Oysters Rockefeller and turtle soup. But the first Foundation presentation in New Orleans was spectacular as Pepe and Domingo both stirred up the crowd.

Shortly thereafter, I met Jorge Mas Canosa and his wife, Irma. Irma would have made an impressive First Lady for a free Cuba.   Cristina and I became good friends with the Mas Canosas. Whenever I invited him to visit us in New Orleans, he would pack the house full of visitors. Few Cuban exiles lived in New Orleans, but it was not uncommon for us to have over 600 people come to listen to Jorge. His energy was spectacular; when he predicted that Fidel would fall, we all believed him. Things might not have turned out quite as he expected, but at the time it was wonderful to hear his inspiring predictions for Cuba's future. And the fact is that Fidel is not immortal. We have the winning hand; sooner or later, Cuba will be free and Jorge's predictions will come true.

Soon after we met, Jorge named me the General Counsel of

the Foundation . As the Foundation's legal advisor, I found myself frequently switching between offensive and defensive roles. Jorge was a disturbing figure for the pro-Castro element in the United States, and the left attacked him unmercifully. In addition, Castro waged war against him from abroad. Cuban agents accused Mas Canosa of terrorism and everything else they could make up.

I met many charismatic individuals when I joined the Foundation. They included Clara del Valle, who now serves as Vice Chairwoman; Pepe Hernández, who is President; and Ninoska Peréz Castellón, a well-known radio and TV commentator who was the voice of the Foundation on radio. Jorge Mas Canosa's son, Jorge Mas Santos joined later, as did Juan Gutierrez, a highly successful New Jersey contractor.

The Foundation was composed of over 170 directors and trustees who annually paid between $5,000 to $10,000 (aside from their political contributions). Many of them were self-made Cuban American millionaires who gave generously to the cause. Among them was Tony Costa, owner of Costa Nursery, who today leads the Foundation for Human Rights in Cuba and provides valuable and needed assistance to the dissidents in the island. He shares that responsibility with Clara's husband, Mario Luis del Valle, who is a board member. The Foundation for Human Rights is spectacular but receives little recognition; typically only the Foundation's political efforts make the papers.

Erelio Peña, a friend of my sister, Lita, was another prominent director who helped introduce me to the Foundation. In Puerto Rico, the Foundation's leadership is headed by Miguel Ángel Martínez, Domingo Sadurní, Severiano López, and Jerónimo Estevez.

In New Jersey, Juan Gutíerrez, Remberto Pérez, and Abel Hernandez lead the organization. A close personal friend, Juan built an enormous construction company, Northeast

Construction Company, which employs nearly 1,000 people. He is charismatic, gregarious, and well liked. As an active Republican, he once hosted George W. Bush in his home. Remberto Peréz is close to Senator Bob Menendez, a Democrat who now wields significant power in the Senate. In New York, a leading figure is Luis Pons, a black Cuban of Asian descent. Charming and disarming, he is sharp as a tack and has built a significant business in healthcare.

Although Jorge created the Foundation with the support of Ronald Reagan, he never hesitated to pit the two parties against each other to get what he wanted. When Cuban American attorney Mario Baeza was about to be nominated as Assistant Secretary of State for Inter-American Affairs, Jorge opposed the nomination and called upon three of his influential Democrat friends: New Jersey Senator Bill Bradley, New Jersey Congressman Robert Torricelli, and Florida Senator Bob Graham. Baeza's name was quickly crossed off the list.

When then-President George H. W. Bush refused to sign a piece of embargo legislation known as the Torricelli-Graham Bill, Jorge Mas Canosa invited Bill Clinton to visit him in Miami at the Versailles Restaurant. It is said that if you want to win the Cuban American vote—and therefore Florida and the Presidency—you better go eat black beans and rice at the Versailles Restaurant on 8th Street (or *Calle Ocho*).

Clinton then attended a Foundation-sponsored fundraiser in Miami's Little Havana and announced, "I have read the Torricelli-Graham Bill, and I like it." Clinton also declared that the Bush Administration "has missed a big opportunity to put the hammer down on Fidel Castro in Cuba." The crowd cheered. Clinton went home $275,000 richer, while President Bush eventually signed the bill.

Unfortunately, that episode led to a very bad relationship between the Bush and the Mas families that continues to this

day. Years after Mas Canosa's death, when it became clear that
Jeb Bush and Jorge Mas Santos were at odds, I arranged for a
meeting to try to calm things down between the families. I went
with Mas Santos and Domingo Moreira to Tallahassee to see
then-Governor Jeb Bush. Domingo, like me, is a staunch
Republican and a good diplomat. Regrettably, the two sons
inherited the enmity that existed between their fathers. The two
had a polite meeting—but the atmosphere was chilly. Years later,
the George W. Bush administration ostracized the Foundation.

Jorge Mas Canosa wanted the Foundation to operate worldwide, and his influence spread far beyond South Miami. In 1986,
the Foundation sponsored a U.S. appearance by Jonas Savimbi,
the head of UNITA, a rebel group backed by the U.S. in the
Angolan Civil War. Castro sent soldiers to Angola to fight on
the side of the government. In 1989, Mas Canosa invited Boris
Yeltsin to visit Miami; a Foundation office was soon opened in
Moscow. In 1990, after Nelson Mandela praised Fidel's Cuba,
Mas Canosa arranged for Cuban exiles to refuse any official welcome to the South African president. Not even Mandela intim-
idated Mas Canosa.

I learned the art of U.S politics on my trips to Washington
with Jorge Mas Canosa. He had a lobbying company that
arranged for him to meet with senators and congressmen. From
time to time, the poor lobbyist, Jonathan Slade, could only
arrange a meeting with an aide. Jorge Mas Canosa would exco-
riate him for his inefficiency, demanding only to meet with the
senators or congressmen themselves.

We literally ran through the halls of Congress to get the
work done; on any given day we would meet with twenty senators and thirty congressmen. Jorge always took the lead in conversation. His passion was so evident that he could persuade
powerful politicians to take action. Through such meetings, he
was able to strengthen and enforce the U.S.–Cuba embargo.

Perhaps our strongest ally in Congress was a Democrat, Senator Robert Torricelli of New Jersey. (After Florida, New Jersey has the largest number of Cuban Americans.) The two often worked together to draft embargo legislation. I walked beside Senator Torricelli during Jorge Mas Canosa's funeral, where he gave a heartfelt eulogy. Another Foundation supporter was Senator Robert Menendez, a Cuban American also from New Jersey.

Jorge Mas Canosa once invited Cristina and me to his home in Key West, where we spent a weekend talking about his plans to bring democracy to Cuba. His son, Jorge Mas Santos, joined us as we laughed and debated some of Mas Canosa's out-of-the-box theories. He wanted to facilitate Chinese immigration to Cuba and bring their enterprising and hardworking spirit to the island. He probed my knowledge of maritime law and pitched his idea of making Cuba a flag of convenience to ensure that the country would have a large fleet of vessels. He was also in favor of a flat tax.

That weekend, Mas Canosa had brought a Cuban ex-boxer to help him with his garden. A huge guy who had eaten one too many black beans, the boxer might have been fast at one time, but that weekend he was slow as molasses. Jorge Mas Canosa bragged about his great worker, but every time I turned around I found him lying down in a hammock. The boxer once complained to me that Jorge seemed to expect the seeds in the garden to flower overnight. I knew he was telling the truth; Jorge was not one for waiting patiently for things to change on their own.

Perhaps Jorge worked so hard because he knew that his days were numbered. I remember going to a mass in Key Largo where the priest prayed for the ailing fifty-eight-year-old Mas Canosa. His life was slipping away. Those were sad days for us. On November 23, 1997, Jorge's death brought an end to the most hopeful years of the movement for freedom in Cuba. Many in the Foundation suspected that Castro's biotechnology was responsible for Mas Canosa's death.

Regrettably, none of us had quite the same combination of skill, passion, and enthusiasm that Jorge brought to the fight. As a director of the Foundation, I stood guard by his casket while over 120,000 people filed by to pay their respects to this formidable man. Many leading politicians and personalities traveled from throughout the United States to attend his funeral. Thousands upon thousands of Cuban exiles were in attendance. We had put our trust in him to free Cuba. God only knows what Cuba would be like if he were alive today.

LECH WALESA AND OMAR LÓPEZ MONTENEGRO

LECH WALESA GLOWED. I KNOW THAT SOUNDS PECULIAR, BUT there appeared to be a white light around his face. I wasn't prepared for that—I expected a tough union leader, the kind of guy who works with his hands. When you got past the glow, you could see that he was a man who had suffered greatly in his life. Walesa had been many things in his life—an electrician, a union leader, a politician. That day, I was meeting with Walesa the human rights activist.

Walesa was born in September 1943. His father, a carpenter, was arrested by the Nazis and thrown into a concentration camp. Walesa was raised by his mother, Feliksa. Tough mothers raise tough sons, and he credits her for his strong Catholicism and undeniable tenacity. Walesa and I instantly hit it off because of our shared Catholic faith.

I knew I was meeting a mystical man. *Time Magazine* named him Man of the Year in 1981. Walesa was awarded the Nobel Peace Prize in 1983. On July 4, 1989, he received the Liberty Medal; that same year, he was also awarded the Presidential Medal of Freedom.

Omar López Montenegro, the leader of the human rights movement of the Foundation, had arranged our meeting in Miami Beach. He knew I wanted to learn how Walesa had triumphed over the communists. Also in attendance was Carlos Saladrigas, a good friend, successful businessman, and Cuban patriot. Saladrigas leads the Cuba Study Program, an elite group of Cuban American intellectuals. He is a staunch opponent of the U.S.-Cuba embargo and believes that we should do away with it.

Walesa arrived in a hotel in Miami Beach with one of his daughters and several aides. He wore on his lapel a badge depicting the Black Madonna, a famous icon of the Virgin Mary and the Christ Child kept in the Czestochowa Monastery near Warsaw. Walesa is deeply devoted to the Virgin Mary and has said many times that she was the key to his faith and work. When he appeared on the cover of *Time Magazine* under the title "Shaking up Communism," you can see the badge.

He also credited the Polish Pope, John Paul II, for his success in bringing down communism in Poland. He was quoted as saying, "Until he became Pope, I had ten members of an independent union in Gdansk; afterwards I had ten million." Thus the glow.

He made clear that his Catholic faith gave him the strength to do what he had accomplished in life—which was quite a lot. He is credited with bringing Poland to democracy. His slogan when he ran for president against the communists was, "*I don't want to, but I've got no choice.*" On December 9, 1990, Walesa became the first democratically elected president of Poland.

I only had one question for Walesa: "How can we free Cuba?" His answer lasted about an hour. He explained to us that we needed to bring the various dissident movements in Cuba into contact with each other. I explained to him that in Cuba, Castro monitors those who can use cell phones and computers, and doesn't allow people to congregate. Years after our meeting, Alan Gross, an American Jew, was arrested and sentenced to fifteen years by Castro for delivering computers to fellow Jews who lived in Cuba.

Walesa also recommended that we organize local opposition and events. When he suggested soccer games, I told him that in Cuba we played baseball, not soccer. He said that would do. His idea was to arrange it so that different dissident groups would attend baseball games and collaborate to topple the Castro regime. This kind of strategy was tried, but so far the most effective group has been the Ladies in White. Their demonstrations have brought many brave Cubans to their aid against Castro, but they pay a heavy price.

Walesa continues to support the cause of Cuban freedom, and he works closely with Omar López Montenegro to help bring this about. Omar is quiet and gentle in person, but he is a very courageous man. In Cuba, he was Secretary General of the Association for Free Art—a non-violent organization that supported freedom of expression in the work of poets, artists, intellectuals, and writers. In 1992, Castro arrested Omar eleven times over a seven-month period and ultimately ejected him from the country as a *persona non grata*.

Omar's official title at the Foundation is Director of the Human Rights. In this capacity, he travels all over the world, overtly and covertly, to denounce the Castro regime. He has spoken repeatedly at the Human Rights Commission of the United Nations. Cuban exiles have no seats at the U.N., so Omar has to make special arrangements with the few countries courageous enough to oppose Castro openly. President Bolaños of Nicaragua allowed him to appear as part of the Nicaraguan Delegation at the Human Rights Commission of the United Nations, where Omar denounced Castro's violations of human rights. A perennial irritant to Castro and his thugs, Omar has also appeared at the European Parliament in Strasbourg and Brussels.

Omar is a frequent visitor at the World Assembly of CIVICUS, an organization comprised of a thousand entities that promote civil society in their countries. The full name is CIVICUS: World Alliance for Citizen Participation. Based in Johannesburg, South Africa, with offices in Washington, D.C.

Omar travels to wherever Castro's enemies can be found. He goes all over the world making alliances with those who oppose dictatorships in favor of democracy and civil society. His latest clandestine trip was to Amman, Jordan, to meet with a group of Middle Eastern activists. Through various media outlets, he makes sure that the world knows about Castro's atrocities.

Under Attack by Castro and the Liberal Media

The following is a poem by Kent M. Keith that hung on the wall of Mother Theresa's home in Calcutta. I read it to the jury during my opening statement in the case of the Cuban *American National Foundation v. Wayne Smith*:

Do It Anyway

People are unreasonable, illogical, and self-centered. Love them anyway.

If you do good, people will accuse you of selfish, ulterior motives. Do good anyway.

If you are successful, you will win false friends and true enemies. Succeed anyway.

The good you do today will be forgotten tomorrow. Do good anyway.

Honesty and frankness make you vulnerable. Be honest and frank anyways.

The biggest people with the biggest ideas can be shot down by the smallest people with the smallest minds. Think big anyway.

People favor underdogs but follow only top dogs. Fight for the underdog anyway.

What you spend years building may be destroyed overnight. Build anyway.

People really need help, but may attack you if you help them. Help people anyway.

Give the world the best you've got and you'll get kicked in the teeth. Give the world the best you've got anyway.

This poem expresses how most of us feel in the exile community. We are struggling to free a country from a dictator, and yet the leftist media pounds us relentlessly. We expected insults and lies from Fidel Castro. He often calls us "terrorists" or the "Miami mafia." We even imagined that misinformed people might believe him. But, incredibly, the mainstream media continues to shamelessly repeat the dictator's words. It might just be ignorance, but often I think that certain members of the media really do hate their own country. They definitely seem to enjoy it when Fidel Castro thumbs his nose at our country.

Eventually, the attacks in the media grew so vicious and false that the only solution was to start filing lawsuits. One day while hunting in Mexico, I received a call from Jorge Mas Canosa. Very upset, he told me that *The New Republic* had called him "a mobster" on its cover and he feared his grandchildren would hear about it. Jorge Mas Santos has a son, "Jorgito," whom Mas Canosa adored. Jorgito is now seventeen and is as charming as his grandfather was. He calls me "Georgefowler," one word.

After evaluating the situation, I advised Jorge Mas Canosa to start suing. He filed suit against *The New Republic*, eventually winning $100,000 and an apology from the magazine. The writer was Ann Louise Bardach, who I encountered again years later during a legal battle against *The New York Times*.

Jorge Mas Canosa believed in fighting back. When the *Miami Herald* advanced pro-Castro views and published outrageous articles against the Cuban exile community, Jorge declared war. He bought billboards on Miami's buses urging people to boycott the Miami Herald and question the truth of its articles. After their circulation and advertising revenue dropped dramatically, the paper cried uncle and worked out a deal with Jorge.

Still the assaults continued—some even showed up on film.

Wayne S. Smith was a professor at John Hopkins University who frequently appeared on television attacking U.S.–Cuba policy. He defended Castro in his interviews. While discussing the Brothers to the Rescue murders, Smith defended Castro and argued that, "the little planes had crossed Cuban territory." In 1992, he gave an interview for a PBS documentary entitled *Campaign for Cuba*.

I filed a defamation suit against Smith in response to lies he told in the documentary. *Campaign for Cuba* reviewed the Foundation's political influence and role in shaping U.S. policy towards Cuba. The defamation occurred during a section that examined the Foundation, Congressman Dante Fascell (a fierce anti-Castro U.S. Congressman), and the Foundation's Political Action Committee (PAC). The documentary stated that, "Representative Fascell was also instrumental in the creation of the congressionally funded National Endowment for Democracy, or NED, . . . which has awarded about $900,000 in grants to the Cuban American National Foundation." The documentary then showed Wayne Smith giving the following statement:

> It's interesting that the National Endowment for Democracy has contributed to the Cuban American National Foundation, and it, in turn, through its, its, its own organization, through its PAC, has contributed to the campaign funds of many Congressmen, including some who have been involved with the National Endowment for Democracy, from whence they got the money in the first place, including Dante Fascell.

I sent Professor Smith a letter asking for a retraction. There was absolutely no connection between the money given to the Foundation by the NED and the money given by individuals from the Foundation to the PAC. Smith's accusation was a blatant lie, and he knew it. Whatever money the Foundation received from the NED was used for its rightful purpose. The PAC contributions came straight from the donators' pockets before going to hundreds of different politicians.

Shortly before the trial, Smith's lawyer, Alfredo Durán, and I had reached compromise language on a retraction. However, the day before the trial was to begin, Alfredo told me that Smith had gotten a call from "Havana" and was going to try the case after all. I interpreted that Fidel wanted Smith to try the case and win it.

In 1996, the highly publicized case went before Judge Thomas Spencer in Miami State Court. The courtroom was packed, and the case was on the front pages of Miami papers every day. More than once, I was physically attacked as I tried to leave the courtroom. Men I believe to have been Castro's agents made their way through the crowd and violently pushed me. During one break, on my way to the courtroom door, a sinister-looking man in dark glasses came straight at me. Roberto Martin Perez, Ninoska' husband, literally picked the man up and threw him away from me, slamming him against the door. Roberto is a very strong man, and I was happy that he was there. Nobody bothered me after that.

This case wasn't about money; we had no desire to profit off of Wayne Smith. We wanted to set the record straight, clear the Foundation's name, and ensure that people would think twice before lying about us. I tried the case, which lasted four days, with my brother-in-law, G. Luis Dominguez. I called Congressman Fascell as a witness to debunk Smith's claims. He was spectacular and the jury soon became enamored with him.

The jury returned a unanimous verdict of $10,000 in nominal damages and three times that in punitive damages, or $30,000. Professor Smith moved for a new trial and a judgment notwithstanding the verdict; Judge Spencer denied both motions. Newspapers and radio stations quickly proclaimed the victory.

Alfredo Durán put up a worthy defense—but to no avail. The trial was costly for my law firm—which, as usual for this kind of work, did it on a pro bono basis—but I felt it was important to correct the record, as did Jorge Mas Canosa and Pepe Hernández.

A year or so later, the decision was reversed on appeal because Judge Spencer had not allowed the entire documentary to be shown. I believe Judge Spencer was right not to have shown the whole thing; it would have been useless and irrelevant. But although we lost the monetary damages, we weren't disappointed—the highly publicized jury verdict was what counted. It wasn't about money. After the trial, Smith suggested that he only lost the case because he had fought the Foundation on their home turf, Miami. However, only two Cuban Americans were on the jury; the rest was made up of an African American, a Nicaraguan, and two Caucasians.

These kinds of cases are very difficult to win, and since the Foundation was deemed a public figure, the standard of proof was even higher. Not only did I have to prove that Smith had lied, I had to prove that he lied with malice. The jury indeed found that Smith had lied maliciously and clearly crossed the line. It is unwise to slander the Foundation and expect to get away with it.

THE EMBARGO AND THE BATTLE FOR CUBA IN WASHINGTON

Regrettably, the embargo on business and travel to Cuba garners more interest in the United States than any other Cuban issue. Regardless of how many people Castro kills or tortures, only the embargo makes the news.

Many liberals believe that the Cuban American community alone is responsible for the embargo, but this is incorrect. Most of us support it, but it is not our policy. The embargo has been the official U.S. government policy throughout many administrations both Republican and Democrat. The leaders in Washington are well aware that Castro's Cuba has always been a terrorist-harboring, anti-American rogue state.

The embargo was imposed in October 1960 after Cuba nationalized U.S. property on the island. In 1992, the embargo was codified into law as the Cuban Democracy Act, also known as the Torricelli Act. Its purpose was to force the Cuban government to move towards democratic government and greater respect for human rights. In 1996, Congress passed the Helms–Burton Act, which restricted United States citizens from doing business in or with Cuba. President Clinton expanded the trade embargo in 1999 by prohibiting foreign subsidiaries of U.S. corporations from trading with Cuba.

Before it was passed, the Helms–Burton Act was in danger of

being defeated in Congress. The European Union opposed the Act because they felt the United States was dictating how other nations ought to conduct their trade. Sadly, Castro's murders actually helped the passage of the bill after the 1996 Brothers to the Rescue shootdown galvanized the nation against Castro. I'll discuss that tragic event later on in the book.

The Foundation played an important role in shaping the embargo legislation that became the Helms-Burton Act and the Torricelli Act. Castro and his allies—along with opportunistic American businessmen and politicians—made relentless efforts to end the embargo. In turn, we worked equally hard to maintain it. We believe that the United States of America should not freely trade with a tyrannical enemy and state sponsor of terrorism. Any business with Cuba would ultimately benefit the dictator alone. Castro runs his country like a feudal state and takes a cut of every transaction. He uses that money to wage war against us and bolster his draconian regime.

Let me give you an example of a typical embargo battle in Washington. In an effort to weaken the U.S. embargo against Cuba, Senator Christopher J. Dodd, a relentless anti-embargo crusader, introduced legislation (the Dodd Amendment) to allow the sale of food and medicine to certain countries, including Cuba. The Dodd Amendment passed, 68–30. We at the Foundation gathered and defined a strategy to undercut the new amendment. We then provided our good friends on the Senate floor with language—sponsored by Senator Robert G. Torricelli (the "Torch")—to exempt all nations on the State Department's list of terrorist states from the amendment. The list included all of our traditional enemies: Cuba, Libya, Syria, Iran, Iraq, and North Korea.

Dodd's target was the embargo on Cuba. Understanding that Torricelli's amendment would gut his legislation and keep the Cuban embargo intact, Dodd tried to table it. His efforts proved unsuccessful. We successfully pushed for the exemption, and the Senate approved the Torricelli Amendment, 67–30.

On the steps outside the Capitol after the vote, Senator Dodd came up to Pepe Hernández and me and said, *"You've won again."*

It wasn't a matter of winning or losing for us. We just didn't want to put more money in Castro's hands.

You should know by now that Fidel Castro doesn't care about the people of Cuba, but know that he has even rejected free food and medicine. On May 15, 1998, Senator Jesse Helms (R-NC), Chairman of the Senate Foreign Relations Committee, and twenty other senators introduced legislation to provide Cubans with $100 million in free food, medicine, and medical equipment. Helms said:

> If Castro allows this food and medicine into Cuba, it will bring relief to millions of Cubans who cannot buy the basic necessities. If he does not allow the food and medicine in, then eleven million Cubans will know exactly who is responsible for their daily suffering.[15]

Helms argued that giving the aid would display the generosity of the American people and their concern for suffering people of Cuba. To prevent Castro from stealing resources, the proposed aid would be channeled through non-government organizations (NGOs) in Cuba and through the Roman Catholic Church.

The news articles reported:

> Helms, after consulting with the leading Cuban exile group, the Cuban American National Foundation, signaled some time ago that he would support direct U.S. assistance provided none of it went through or to Castro government officials.

---

[15] Sen. Jesse Helms. "The Cuban Solidarity Act of 1998." *Congressional Record* 144: 7 (May 14, 1998) p. 9,258.

We worked hand in hand with Senator Jesse Helms to bring the aid program to fruition. Although elderly, he was charismatic and worked like the Energizer Bunny—he just kept going and going and going. I admired this great American. Castro's response to our offer—to give his people help they badly needed—was typical. Take the headline in the *World News*, May 16, 1998: "Helms' Cuban Aid Bill 'Diabolical,' Castro Says."

The proud and well-fed Castro denounced Helms's proposal as "humiliating and absolutely unacceptable. This aid won't enter Cuba because we have a government with a sense of honor," Castro said. Personal honor versus the Cuban people's hunger—which do you think mattered more to Castro? He claimed that the offer was "something diabolical invented after the Pope's visit." Castro rejected the aid. Socialist governments want the people to be thankful only to their dictator.

I have met with many of the country's most influential politicians on behalf of Cuba. I have had brief meetings with George W. Bush, George H. W. Bush, and even met President Obama. I have known Jeb Bush for many years. His sons are friendly with members of my family. I don't think there is anyone in the Republican Party today who understands Cuba better than him. He is married to a Mexican American and understands the Latin community. I stay in touch with Jeb and have encouraged him to run for President. Unlike Romney, he will know how to get the Latin vote.

Through the Mas family, I met Marco Rubio and have had brief exchanges with him. I am a fan. Once when our now indicted, idiot, former Mayor of New Orleans, Ray Nagin, visited Cuba to "study hurricane response" Marco lambasted him in a letter. I thanked Marco personally. Nagin claimed that unlike the people of New Orleans the Cuban people obeyed the evacuation orders. I explained to the press that he was right, otherwise they would be shot.

Jeb and Marco stick together and have been supporting each other for the past few years. I think that either of them would be terrific as President of the United States.

Outside of Florida, I am in close contact and have a good relationship with Louisiana Senators Mary Landrieu (D-LA) and David Vitter (R-LA). Mississippi Governor Haley Barbour and I once spent four days discussing Cuba at length at a club in California.

I am a big fan of Rudy Giuliani and strongly supported his bid for the presidency. Jorge Mas Santos and I met with Rudy in Lafayette, Louisiana, to discuss Cuba. Rudy really understands the issue well. I also met with Senator McCain several times over the years and can say that he has the right intentions for Cuba. I supported his bid for the presidency, but unfortunately his campaign was a disaster.

I was one of ten in the national Hispanic steering committee for Mitt Romney, *Juntos Con Romney*. That team included Marco Rubio and Carlos Gutierrez, a former U.S. Secretary of Commerce. Gutierrez, a fellow Cuban American, really understands the challenge that Republicans face in courting Hispanics. Frankly, Romney did not listen to our recommendations. I wrote a paper for Romney at his request, but I believe the anti-immigration forces in the party held him captive. We won't have a Republican president until we get past those forces. Carlos Gutierrez and I are separately working on that initiative.

Twice I had the privilege of meeting with former President Jimmy Carter at the Carter Center to discuss Cuba. The only Cuban issue he had focused on as president was the U.S. embargo. We spent several hours politely arguing. His goal was to get the Foundation to support his wish to end the U.S. embargo. I told him I would put the embargo on the table—so long as he would consider prosecuting Castro for his crimes against humanity. Carter initially agreed, but his allies who supported lifting the sanctions violently opposed the idea. You see, this group often visited Cuba to meet with Fidel—and it would have been impolite to support his indictment. Our discussions soon ground to a halt.

I have met with a number of world figures on the Cuba issue, including President Aznar of Spain and Presidents Aleman and Bolaños from Nicaragua. I have had the privilege of playing host to Oscar Arias—the former President of Costa Rica and Nobel Peace Prize winner at home—and Gonzalo Sánchez de Lozada—the former President of Bolivia. I am also friends with Jose Rizo, the former Vice President of Nicaragua. Pedro Rossello, the Governor of Puerto Rico, had his administration hire me to handle the oil spill disaster that occurred in 1994 off the beaches of San Juan, Puerto Rico.

Let me give an idea of the work we do. On July 15 1998, other Foundation members and I traveled to Washington for a two-day trip, seeking support for our anti-Castro efforts. During that brief period of time, we met with the following senators: Senator Peter Fitzgerald (R-IL), Senator Lott (R-MS), Senator McConnell (R-MS), Senator Larry Craig (R-ID), Senator Robert Torricelli (D-NJ), Senator Frank Murkowski (R-AK), Senator Conrad Burns (R-MT), Senator Robert Bennett (R-UT), Senator Ben Campbell (R-CO), Senator Kent Conrad (D-ND), Senator John McCain (R-AZ), Senator Wayne Allard (R-CO), Senator Richard Bryan (D-NV), Senator Mary Landrieu (D-LA), and Senator Sam Brownback (R-KS).

As you can clearly see, we take the cause seriously!

THE HUNT FOR FIDEL CASTRO

EVER SINCE CASTRO SEIZED POWER, CUBAN EXILES HAVE CONSTANTLY sought his indictment and prosecution in a court of law. We have tried to indict the dictator in Chile, Costa Rica, Argentina, Colombia, Santo Domingo, Spain, and the U.S. The Foundation has made joint efforts with other exile groups to bring him to justice; Foundation President Francisco "Pepe" Hernández has been particularly active in this respect. Our legal team has filed criminal actions against him in any foreign countries we knew he was visiting.

Castro has supported violent terrorist movements throughout Central and South America. In January 1989, armed militants in Argentina brutally attacked a fort in the La Tablada area of Buenos Aires. Thirty-nine people died in the assault. After many of the assailants—part of a group called "All For the Fatherland"—were arrested, the Foundation paid lawyers and pressed for Argentinean prosecutors to review the case. Our investigation traced the attack to Cuban training and support.

In 1984, the contra leader Eden Pastor—also known as Commander Zero—bombed a press conference in Costa Rica. The bombing resulted in the murders of three journalists, including an American, Linda Fraser. The Foundation offered legal expertise to the journalists who investigated the horrible incident.

In Chile, the father of a victim of Castro's terrorism filed a criminal claim against the dictator. The claim asserted that Castro supported murder, the training of terrorist groups, and the importation of illegal weapons to Chile. Its purpose was to prevent Castro from attending the inauguration ceremony of Chilean President Ricardo Lagos.

You may wonder why the U.N. never acted against Castro when they intervened in places like Yugoslavia, Rwanda, Sierra Leone, and Cambodia. The answer is simple: much of the U.N. supports Castro because of their anti-U.S. bias. Believe it or not, Cuba actually has a seat on the 47-member U.N. Human Rights Council—the body responsible for addressing human rights violations.

THE CRIMINAL COMPLAINT IN SPAIN, THE *QUERELLA*

THE AUDIENCIA NACIONAL IS A SPANISH CRIMINAL COURT THAT investigates claims of terrorism and corruption. The judges of this court are independent and claim to have worldwide jurisdiction. Judge Baltasar Garzón was its most prominent judge. A friend of Fidel Castro, Garzón loves publicity and views himself as a legal toreador. Perhaps at one time he was the most famous judge in the world. We have tangled.

Recently, however, Garzón strayed too close to the horns. The rogue judge refused to accept any limitations on his authority. Garzón was convicted in Spain for several crimes and suspended from judicial activity. No longer a judge, he is counsel to Julian Assange of WikiLeaks.

Garzón's anti-U.S. views are obvious. He sought to criminally investigate former U.S. Secretary of State Henry Kissinger and pushed for the indictment of former Bush Administration officials for supporting torture. Also included in his list of targets was Alberto González, the former U.S. Attorney General.

In 1998, Garzón accepted a criminal complaint against Chile's former president, Augusto Pinochet, who was living in England. He demanded Pinochet's extradition to Spain to face charges for torture and conspiracy that occurred during his presidency. An English court accepted Garzón's ruling, despite the fact that Pinochet was eighty-three and very ill at the time. Leftists welcomed this legal action and hailed Garzón as a hero. He is no hero.

A defiant Pinochet claimed that he was not guilty of any crimes and that Garzón's charges were politically motivated. While I will not opine on Pinochet's guilt here, I can assure you that Garzón had political intentions.

When he brought charges against Pinochet Garzón claimed that the *Audiencia Nacional* had worldwide jurisdiction. When we at the Foundation saw this filing, it occurred to us that "what is good for the goose is good for the gander." Knowing full well that the *Audiencia Nacional* leaned far to the left, we took the Pinochet *Querella* (criminal complaint) and substituted his name with the names of Fidel Castro Ruz, Raúl Castro Ruz, Osmani Cienfuegos, and Carlos Amat. We retained Spanish counsel to help.

The Foundation undertook a massive effort to collect affidavits from family members of those who Castro murdered, tortured, and psychologically abused. After we publicly notified the Cuban exile community about the effort, hundreds of people promptly arrived at our offices. They formed a line that went for blocks and stood for hours in the sweltering Miami heat. Old men and women in wheelchairs and walkers were among the many who came to testify.

It was an emotional time for us at the Foundation. People cried as they told us their horror stories of Castro's inhumanity and abuse. We had to ask for volunteers to help us handle all the affidavits. It was a 'round-the-clock operation. Pepe Hernández, Clara del Valle, Laly Sampedro, Ninoska Pérez, and many others did everything they could to obtain the evidence. We weren't filing some frivolous lawsuit to seek publicity; we were gathering the hard evidence we needed to bust Castro and his thugs for good either in Spain or elsewhere. Once the herculean evidence-gathering campaign was complete, we presented the *Querella before the*

Juzgado Central de Instruccion de la Audiencia Nacional in Spain.

The *Querella* was very lengthy and detailed. The lead plaintiff was the Foundation for Human Rights in Cuba, an organization of the Foundation. The affidavit found that since 1959, more than 500,000 Cubans went through Castro's prisons and the concentration camps—an amazing number considering that in 1960 the population was only seven million.

The plea cites evidence that between 15,000 and 17,000 people were shot by Castro's men (although even more were murdered by other means). One example was Humberto Sori Marin, a forty-six-year-old lawyer and newspaper man. He was shot on April 20, 1961, shortly after he was injured while being apprehended. Castro himself lied to Marin's mother to her face telling her that her son would not be executed. He was already dead.

The *Querella* detailed the organizations created by Fidel Castro to repress the fundamental rights and liberties of his countrymen. Castro neutralized all the organizations of power that might have competed with him, such as the army, the unions, student and professional organizations, the press, and all religious institutions. He took total control and implemented what we called *revolutionary terror.*

We described the various institutions that Castro implemented to maintain his power and continues to use to this day. Castro's primary instrument of terror is the *Ministerio del Interior* (MININT). The MININT directs and controls all other repressive organizations in the Castro regime. Its agents detain and question anybody who might oppose the regime, often with the ultimate goal of killing them. The organization spreads terror in the hearts of the Cuban people. One branch of MINIT, the Department of Security, is known by Cubans as the "Red Gestapo."

Another apparatus of repression is the *Dirección General de la Inteligencia* (DGI). Its job is to collect information and engage in international espionage and counter-espionage. It also tries to repress and control Cubans who travel and live outside of Cuba. DGI agents have infiltrated foreign governments and Cuban exile organizations.

Also denounced in the *Querella* was *La Unidad Militar de Ayuda a la Producción* (UMAP)—"United Military to Help in Production." The name is misleading; UMAP has nothing to do with production. Instead, it administers the concentration camps where all those who Castro considers "inferior"—due to ideology, sex, or religion—are imprisoned. Included are thousands of Catholics, Protestants, Jehovah's Witnesses, and homosexuals.

Castro's government tried to "reform" so-called social deviants through "military discipline," i.e., ill treatment, starvation, and isolation. Many of those thrown into the camps committed suicide. Castro's blatant homophobia and anti-gay views are no secret. In fact, he even declared that there are no homosexuals in Cuba.

The next organization listed was the *Departamento Técnico de Investigaciones* (DTI)—the Technical Department of Investigations. They carried out the torture of political and non-political prisoners in Cuba's jails. Captives were beaten and subjected to psychological experiments. The DTI practiced all kinds of torture, both physical and psychological, followed by medical treatment and drugs to prolong the suffering.

Probably the most infamous organizations in Cuba are the *Comités de Defensa de la Revolución* (CDR)—the Committees for the Defense of the Revolution. They act as Castro's secret police. On every block there is a CDR whose job is to spy on every home. CDR agents demand total obedience to Castro's dictatorship; they eavesdrop on conversations and prohibit people from talking to each other on the streets. They routinely interrogate people about the activities of family members and friends.

CASTRO'S PRISONS

The *QUERELLA* ALSO DETAILED THE HORRORS OF CASTRO'S prisons. Wherever we could, we named the wardens so that their actions would never be forgotten. One of the more infamous prisons, Kilo 5.5, was under the direction of one Captain González, nicknamed *El Ñato* (means "flat nose"). The guards at Kilo 5.5 were famous for using sleep deprivation techniques, threatening family members, and extorting visitors. My mother-in-law, Mercedes Jenkins, experienced this treatment when trying to visit her husband in prison.

Kilo 7, in the province of Camaguey, was one of the more violent prisons. In 1974, political prisoners there protested their conditions by going on a hunger strike. Castro's guards attacked, murdering forty helpless people. Perhaps the most famous prison was La Cabaña Fortress, a former Spanish fortress that had dungeons infested with rats. Over one hundred political prisoners were killed there in 1988.

At the G-2 prison of Santiago de Cuba, the cells were kept either at very high or very low temperatures. The prisoners were stripped of their clothes and thrown into isolation chambers. The guards would wake them every twenty minutes after they fell asleep. After a period of time, this torture caused them irreversible psychological damage.

Prisoners were stuffed in cells far beyond the space's capacity. The punishment cells were particularly horrendous. The Foundation created true-to-life replicas of these cells, which I exhibited at the World Trade Center in New Orleans. People were shocked.

The guards altered the configuration of the cells depending upon the torture they wanted to inflict. Cells were kept very hot in summer and very cold in the winter, and there was never any concern for cleanliness or hygiene. Prison guards regularly withheld food, water, and medical assistance from their captives. In the prison of Boniato, many of the prisoners swelled up due to vitamin deficiencies before dying of hunger. Tío Alberto told me that excrement covered the floor in most of the cells where he was put.

After he was freed, Tío Alberto eventually became New Orleans' Director of International Affairs. One night at the World Trade Center, a Cuban with a strong affinity for Castro (he is an agent who organizes trips to Cuba) told my uncle that Castro's prisons were "quite adequate." Tío Alberto decked him to the floor of the Plimsoll Club. It's safe to say that he disagreed with this man's assessment.

The *Querella* described certain cells called the tapiadas, which means "walled-in." They are veritable tombs where the prisoners are kept for months in complete darkness. Some of the smallest are called "shelves" because the prisoner can neither lie down nor stand up. In the prison of *Tres Macíos de Oriente*, prisoners are kept in steel cages without water or toilets.

Political prisoners are frequently thrown together with the criminally and mentally ill. In order not to be assaulted or raped by psychopaths, political prisoners would sometimes scrub themselves with excrement. You might recall the Mariel boatlift of 1980, when Castro shipped thousands of Cuba's common prisoners and lunatics from his insane asylums to the United States along with other exiles. President Carter did not retaliate.

THE WOMEN PRISONERS
OF CUBA

CASTRO'S REPRESSIVE REGIME WAS PARTICULARLY HARSH ON women. The *Querella* noted that as many as 3,000 women were imprisoned in the Potosi Camp of Victoria de las Tunas. Castro's sadistic goons subjected their female prisoners to many humiliations. For example, before being allowed to go to the showers, women were forced to disrobe in front of their captors. Many were beaten and raped by the guards.

Manolo Martínez, the former Chief of Prisons in Guanajay, said this about the Cuban women prisoners: "When these women leave these prisons, they will come out on four legs." Each woman prisoner has her own tragic story. The *Querella* details two such stories.

María Elena Cruz Varela stated that on November 19, 1991, Castro's agents broke into her house. They beat her and forced down five flights of stairs, grabbing her by the throat, repeatedly kicking her, and showering her with obscenities. Her two young children were beaten as well. Once on the street, she was forced to swallow her own writings. On November 21, 1991, the government took her to the prison at Villa Maristas, where she was subjected to constant physical and psychological torture. Ultimately, she was sentenced to two years in jail and tortured for six months straight.

Caridad Roque Pérez made a statement for the *Querella* as well. Condemned to twenty years in prison, she was ultimately sent to the *tapiada*. She was stuffed with two others into a tiny concrete cell with a hermetically sealed metal door. The toilet there was nothing but a small hole in the ground; to use it, you had to bend your knees, crouch over the hole, and hope that no rats jumped out and bit you. One time the hole started gushing sewage. Although they yelled to be let out, the excrement eventually reached their knees. They were kept that way for nearly two days before being taken to a different *tapiada*. The three cellmates took turns sleeping on the concrete floor because there was room for only one to sleep. The other two would crouch against the wall.

Cari elaborated on the *tapiada* cells in Guanabacoa, saying, "The *tapiadas* of Guanabacoa have the particularity that they are underground. Yes, they are underground, exactly under Gallery No. 4, underground at a significant depth without any ventilation, with indescribable humidity. That is why they call them 'the wells.'"

Cari was a beautiful woman who, like many young people of her generation, believed in Castro's revolution. At nineteen she was already an accomplished actress, radio broadcaster, and TV personality at CMQ, a well-known Cuban station. She studied journalism and once acted in a famous play called *Los Malditos*.

Cari's support of the revolution did not last long. Immediately after Castro's violent triumph, she realized the price paid by those who refused to obey his demands. Cari soon met two women who shared her views: Margot Rosello and her sister, Mercedes. The three women formed a team and began to perpetrate acts of sabotage against the Castro dictatorship. They provided support to the anti-Castro guerillas who hid in the Sierra Maestra and El Escambry.

After the women had carried out a number of actions against

Castro, they allowed a man named Pepe Silva to join the group. Cari soon suspected that he was a Castro spy, but Mercedes passionately defended him and swore that he was on their side. Sure enough, he was a rat. On the day of the Bay of Pigs invasion, Mercedes suffered from an extra-uterine pregnancy. When Cari and Margot went to the Sacred Heart Clinic to support her, the three women were apprehended. Cari was devastated. They had been ready to support the invasion force, but now all was lost.

The three women were taken to MINFARN, where they met the infamous *Barba Roja* (red beard) Piñeiro. Cari found out that the traitor Pepe Silva had given Castro's thugs their names quite some time before. Her guards whispered her threatening slogans: "*Paredón, paredón, para saya y pantalón.*" ("The wall, the wall, for the skirt and for the pants.")

The *Barba Roja* threw a number of photographs at Cari that Pepe Silva had taken of her as she was transferring weapons. He demanded that she confess to being the one in the photographs. Cari was wearing the same glasses in the photographs that she wore during the interrogation, but she nevertheless denied the accusation. The situation was very precarious because she was being tried without a trial. Cari said the following:

"In those days of the Bay of Pigs, the *paredón* did not cease to function. Any prisoner you meet today who was in La Cabaña at that time will tell you that they would go to the galleries, point and say, 'You, you, and you,' without trial or anything. But the same was happening in any of the police stations, including the MINFARN."

Cari was subjected to relentless, never-ending interrogations. The guards wouldn't let her sleep and left her alone in a cold cell for hours at a time. The worst of her interrogators was an outrageous man named Idelfonso Canales, who tortured her and promised to kill her father unless she gave them information. After her release, Cari felt some relief when she learned that Canales was later executed for currency trafficking.

Cari's parents assumed that she had been murdered, but after a month they were finally allowed to visit her. They were given only fifteen minutes together. Cari noted that her mother was mentally devastated and that her father looked like a very old man. In that one month, his hair had turned entirely white; it was as if his life had been stolen from him. When her parents asked her about the accusations, she confessed that she was guilty and expected to be there for many years.

On September 22, 1961, Cari was sentenced. The judge and the prosecutor were a perfect combination. Judge Pelayito *"Paredón"* and Flores Ibarra ran a kangaroo court that relished handing out death sentences. Out of the 110 people accused that day, Pelayito and Ibarra quickly secured the death sentence for Cari, Mercedes, Margot, and eighteen men. Shortly after the sentencing, the convicted men were shot in *el paredón*.

Almost four hundred family members were at the scene. Cari described it as pandemonium. Prisoners begged to hug their loved ones for the last time, but their requests were denied. Castro's policemen used the butts of their rifles to strike the prisoners as they reached for their children. Mercedes lost consciousness and had to be taken out in a stretcher.

Cari sat next to a young man named Angel Polin Posada Gutiérrez. Full of life, this young man had been a revolutionary and an ex-captain of Castro's rebel forces. His wife, Norma Albuerne, was also a prisoner and stood in the front line. She was three months pregnant. As he was sentenced to die, Polin grabbed Cari's hand. Squeezing it hard, he told her, "The only thing I ask of you, Cari, is that you take care of her and that my son be born in a free country." Polin tried to run towards Norma, but they dragged her away. He was restrained and led to *el paredón* to die.

Cari's family was there too. She will never forget her father's face at that time. Unable to help his daughter, he balled his hands into fists and bit his lip in sheer desperation. The image has stayed with her for life. My mother later told me that when she left Cuba, Castro's thugs groped her as they patted her down. My grandfather was forced to witness his daughter being abused. Powerless to stop them, he cried out in rage.

Ultimately, Cari, Mercedes, and Margot's life sentences were reduced to twenty years. Cari eventually obtained a humanitarian visa to come to the United States. After hearing the news that his daughter had been set free, her father was so surprised that he suffered a heart attack. When Cari first saw her parents in Miami, she understood how deeply the cruelty of the Castro regime had affected the families of the prisoners. Her mother was no longer the happy, sweet, and caring person that she once knew. The tragedy had warped her.

Although she had been forced to leave Cuba, Cari's mother blamed herself for abandoning her daughter in jail. In her unstable mental condition, she grabbed a knife and tried to kill her husband and herself. After being restrained, she spent five years in an insane asylum. The father survived but was paralyzed after suffering a stroke. He lived with Cari until his death.

Cari has spent her life raising public awareness of Castro's crimes. After her release, she worked with the Foundation for many years as a radio commentator.

It was terribly difficult for me to write these stories. I know Cari and Miñon. These are good women from decent families. They and their families didn't deserve this.

One of the most renowned and courageous Cuban exile women is Miñon Medrano. In her book *Todo Lo Dieron Por Cuba (They Gave it All for Cuba)*[16], she tells the stories of the women who fought against Castro and the suffering they endured. I was

[16]Miñon Medrano, *Todo Lo Dieron Por Cuba* (Fundación Nacional Cubano Americana, 1995).

honored to receive a copy with Miñon's personal dedication to Cristina and me. The book is in Spanish, but I wish it were in English so I could share it with more people. It truly displays the courage of the Cuban women.

In Miñon's book, Cari reflects on her imprisonment: *"We were a generation that was cut off and surrounded, but that gave it all it had. Because we defended Cuba, we lost it all: families, professions, the opportunity to be mothers. But for my country I would do it all over again."*

Cari's story reminded me of Mercedes Jenkins, my mother-in-law. Mercedita had her own Sophie's Choice to make. On the one hand, she could send her four little girls to the United States—to an unknown land, alone, without money or even the ability to speak the language. On the other hand, she feared that if she kept them in Cuba, they would be sent to Russia. She chose to stay behind and send her girls—alone—to freedom in the United States. That is a decision that no mother should have to make.

She smuggled her husband food in jail and tried everything she could to get him out. Although she ultimately succeeded, her daughters felt the consequences. I will not speak to that. I never heard Mercedita defend her decision, but with me she would never have had to. Today, it is the women of Cuba who lead the fight against Castro on his home turf. The wives, mothers, and sisters of the Cuban political prisoners formed a group known as *Las Damas de Blanco*—The Ladies in White. Their courage is unquestionable. Every Sunday after church, the *Damas de Blanco*, parade through the streets of Cuba dressed in white, holding a flower in their hands. And every Sunday, they are beaten by Castro's thugs. I discuss them in detail in a later chapter.

THE BAY OF PIGS

THE QUERELLA EXAMINED ONE OF THE MANY HORRIFIC INCIDENTS that occurred during the Bay of Pigs. 149 captured prisoners were transported from *Playa Girón* (The Bay of Pigs) to the *Palacio de los Deportes de La Habana* (the Havana Sports Palace) to be jailed. They were stuffed into a hermetically sealed truck container and could not breathe. When Commander Osmani Cienfuegos heard their suffocated screams, he said, "It's better. This way we don't have to shoot them."

The truck traveled for eleven hours before reaching its destination. During that entire time, the prisoners did not stop yelling and begging for the doors to be opened. Although the truck drivers made several stops, at no time did they open the doors. By the time the journey ended, the following captured prisoners were dead: Alfredo Cervantes, René Silva Soublette, José Millán, Santos Gil Ramos, Herminio Quintana, Moises Santana, José Villarello, Pedro Rojas, and José Ignacio Macia, a friend of my family.

THE SINKING OF THE TUG *13 DE MARZO*

THE QUERELLA DETAILED THE SINKING OF THE TUG *13 DE MARZO* BY the Cuban government on July 13, 1994. Of the seventy-two people who tried to escape Cuba on the boat, forty-two were killed, including a newborn baby and twenty-two children between five and ten years old.

At 3:15 a.m., the tug *13 de Marzo*, under the command of Captain Fidelio Raynel Prieto, left the Port of Havana. When Prieto exited the bay, one of Castro's fireboats came by and attacked the tugboat with powerful water hoses. Women took their children in their arms and went to the tugboat's deck so that those aboard the fireboat would realize whom they were firing on. The attack continued. Those onboard the tug yelled and begged for them to stop. There was no response. The powerful force of the water hoses sprayed many of the passengers overboard into the sea. Prieto maneuvered to protect them but was helpless to stop the systematic attack.

Two more of Castro's boats showed up and joined in the assault, forcing the tug far into the ocean. Once the thugs believed that they were at a sufficient distance away from the coast, they redoubled their attack. First, the three boats rammed the tug on its port side in an attempt to flip it over, but the tug stayed afloat due to the weight of the people onboard. One of the fireboats then moved to the bow of the tug as another moved to the stern. They battered the tug until it broke in two and sank.

This did not end the atrocity. Children were screaming, but the three attacking fireboats increased their speed—drowning many in the whirlpools that formed in their wake. Forty-two were killed. The thirty-one survivors were arrested and taken to the prison in Villa Marista, La Habana.

Castro's radio stations claimed that the tugboat sank simply because it was old and unseaworthy. Others falsely reported that the tug had accidently collided with one of the other boats. Finally, after much international pressure, Raúl Castro gave an official government speech. He called the incident an accident and declared that the U.S. government was to blame. He said that the U.S. needed to be held accountable for its permanent aggressive attitude towards Castro's Cuba.

Following is a list of those who perished and those who survived:

Perished

Leonardo Notario Gongora, 27
Caridad Leyva Tacoronte, 4
Marjolis Méndez Tacoronte, 17
Pilar Almanza Romero, 30
Manuel Gayol, 58
Helen Martínez Henríquez, 6 months
Xindy Fernández Rodríguez, 2
Yaltamira Anaya-Carrasco, 22
Joel García Suárez, 24
Elio Juan Gutiérrez García, 10
Ernesto Alfonso Loureiro, 25
Augusto Guillermo Guerra Martínez, 45
Lissette María Álvarez Guerra, 24

Julia Caridad Ruiz Blanco, 35
Jorge Arquimedes Lebrigio Flores, 28
Eduardo Suárez Esquivel, 35
Eliecer Suárez Esquivel, 11
Miralis Fernán Rivero, 27
Marta Caridad Tacoronte Vega, 33
Yousel Eugenio Pérez Tacoronte, 11
Odalys Muñoz Garcías, 21
Yasse Perodin Almanza, 11
Yuliana Enríquez Carrazana, 23
Reinaldo Marrero, 48
José Carlos Nikel Anaya, 3
Marta Carrasco Tamayo, 45
Mario Gutiérrez, 35
Fidelio Ramel Prieto Hernández, 50
Lazaro Borges Briel, 34
Armando González Raíz, 50
Giselle Borges Álvarez, 4
Angel René Abreu Ruiz, 3
Estrella Suárez Esquivel, 45
Omar Rodríguez, 30
Yolindis Rodríguez Rivero, 2

Survivors

Mayda Tacoronte Vega, 28
Roman Lugo Martínez, 29
Darney Estevez Martínez, 3
Jorge Alberto Hernández, 32
Modesto Almanza Romero, 28
Sergio Perodin Pérez, 7
Daniel González Hernández, 23
José Fabian Valdes, 17

Yandi Gustavo Martínez Hidalgo, 9
María Victoria García Suárez, 34
Ivan Prieto Suárez, 28
Milena Labrada Tarcoronte, 3
Daisy Martínez Fundora, 26
Susana Roca Martínez, 8
Raúl Muñoz García, 22
Janette Hernández Gutiérrez, 19
Juan Fidel González Salinas, 35
Juan Gustavo Varsaga del Pino, 36
Eugenio Fuentes Díaz, 29
Reinaldo Marrero, Jr., 16
Daniel Prieto Suárez, 28
Jorge Luis Cuba Suárez, 24

THE INTERNATIONAL IMPACT
OF THE *QUERELLA*

IN ADDITION TO ITS ACCOUNT OF THE HORRORS COMMITTED BY
Castro's government, the *Querella* demanded that various government bodies, including the CIA and FBI, produce documents
regarding the accusations. Spanish newspapers picked up the
story after the claim was filed, and Pepe and Clara both went to
Spain and held press conferences. As always, the Spaniards were
divided: half of them thought Castro should be brought to justice while the other half disagreed. In the United States, the
Miami Herald published an editorial entitled "Arrest Castro,
Too." The *Herald* ran a subtitle that said:

Justice in Spain
Dictator Should be Held Accountable for Abusing Basic
Human Rights.

Although the Cuban government called the Querella a
"ridiculous tale," the document received worldwide media attention. Even *The New York Times* favorably alluded to the claim in
an editorial:

If Britain allows Augusto Pinochet to be extradited to
Spain to stand trial for atrocities committed under his

seventeen-year rule, desperate elsewhere will take note: if Mr. Pinochet cannot escape the long arm of international-al law, they might not either.

We certainly agreed. The editorial continued:

Will this justice be truly universal? Conservative critics have seized on the Pinochet case as evidence that human rights groups have a liberal bias: if Mr. Pinochet, why not Fidel Castro? If you want to prosecute bad guys on the right, how about bad guys on the left? Our response is, absolutely. Mr. Castro could be guilty of crimes against humanity in his execution of hundreds, if not thousands of enemies of his Cuban revolution in the early 1960s.

On November 19, 1998, the *Audiencia Nacional* rejected the Querella, concluding that the events it described could not be considered criminal acts constituting genocide, terrorism, or torture. It also found that the acts were not within Spanish juris-diction or the jurisdiction of the *Audiencia Nacional*. Therefore, the court refused to admit the *Querella* against Fidel Castro and his cronies. The decision was signed by Judge Ismael Moreno Chamorro. Although we expected this result, it was very disap-pointing nonetheless. But it was worth it to let the world know about Castro's crimes.

THE FOUNDATION'S BATTLES
WITH *THE NEW YORK TIMES*

I HAVE A FILE ON *THE NEW YORK TIMES* THAT IS TWO INCHES thick. Describing this newspaper as anti-Cuban American would be a huge understatement. Although the paper's writers are mostly competent, they frequently distort the truth with their liberal political views. Over the years, they have consistently displayed great animosity towards Cuban Americans.

If any single publication was responsible for Castro's victory in 1959, it was *The New York Times*. Herbert Matthews, a *New York Times* reporter, made Castro a folk hero in Cuba and worldwide. Matthews described Castro's charisma in drooling terms—naturally failing to note that he was a murderer and a communist.

The New York Times' coverage of Cuban issues has been nothing short of outrageous. Here is an example. Their report on the sinking of the *13 de Marzo*, when Castro's military vessels killed forty-two men, women, and children, was pathetic. This was an act of pure evil that the world needed to know about. Yet on July 24, 1994, *The New York Times* published the story from the perspective of *Granma*, the official newspaper of the Cuban Communist Party. This is the entire *Times* article on the horrific, cruel event:

"Moving to counter accusations about the sinking of a

boat, the Communist Party newspaper *Granma* said today that 32 Cubans drowned after a tugboat they had stolen collided with another Cuban boat.

"The article blamed the accident on those aboard the tugboat, all of whom were attempting to flee Cuba. The report said a total of 63 people set out from Havana before dawn on July 12 in a stolen, leaking wooden tugboat.

"The stolen tug was pursued out of the port first by one and then by two other vessels that used fire hoses to try to stop the tug, *Granma* said. When the pursuing vessels surrounded the stolen tug seven miles north of Havana, one of them collided with its stern and the stolen tug sank within minutes, it said.

"The victims included many women and children. It was the worst incident recorded involving Cubans trying to leave the island illegally.

"The *Granma* report, which made frequent mention of the poor condition of the stolen tugboat, was clearly aimed at countering suggestions that the sinking was deliberate.

"The Cuban authorities had already said that 31 people were rescued after the boat capsized. They had not disclosed the number of people originally on board, however.

"*Granma*'s article, which quoted several survivors of the disaster, accused those who stole the boat of being responsible for the loss of lives."

Despite Castro's verified reputation as a brutal dictator, *The New York Times* printed his version of the events, not the true story. They sided with the murderer not the victims. But when it came to the Foundation, a falsified, hostile story made the

Sunday and Monday front page. *The New York Times* prints stories consistent with their agenda, regardless of whether they are consistent with the truth.

The New York Times has published many negative articles against the Foundation, but two were especially egregious. The first was the front-page Sunday story on July 12, 1998, titled: "Key Cuba Foe Claims Exiles' Backing." The second article was printed the next day under the title: "Life in the Shadows, Trying to Bring Down Castro." The purported co-authors of the articles were Ann Louise Bardach and Larry Rohter.

The first article had a picture of Jorge Mas Canosa, Fidel Castro, and Luis Posada Carriles under this caption: "Luis Posada Carriles, bottom right, who has waged a campaign aimed at toppling Fidel Castro, says Jorge Mas Canosa, top left, and other Cuban American exile leaders gave him money over the years." The article began as follows:

A Cuban exile who has waged a campaign of bombings and assassination attempts aimed at toppling Fidel Castro says that his efforts were supported financially for more than a decade by the Cuban-American leaders of one of America's most influential lobbying groups.

The exile, Luis Posada Carriles, said he organized the wave of bombings in Cuba last year at hotels, restaurants and discotheques, killing an Italian tourist and alarming the Cuban government. Mr. Posada was schooled in demolition and guerilla warfare by the Central Intelligence Agency in the 1960s.

In a series of tape-recorded interviews at a walled Caribbean compound, Mr. Posada said the hotel bombings and other operations had been supported by leaders of the Cuban American National Foundation. Its founder and head, Jorge Mas Canosa, who died last year, was embraced at the White House by Presidents Reagan, Bush and Clinton.

At over ninety years old, Luis Clemente Faustino Posada Carriles—also known as Bambi—is still making headlines. The governments of Venezuela and Cuba declared him a terrorist and accused him of masterminding various terrorist activities. In 2005, Venezuela unsuccessfully tried to have him deported from the United States.

Posada Carriles believes that military action is the only way to eliminate Castro. He supported and trained the original Bay of Pigs invaders. Afterwards, in 1962, he trained at Fort Benning, Georgia. Declassified U.S. documents show that he worked as an agent of the CIA between 1960 and 1976. The Venezuelan and Cuban governments accused him of perpetrating the 1976 bombing of Cuban Airlines Flight 455, which killed seventy-three people. He was imprisoned in Venezuela between 1976 and 1985, but managed to escape.

According to the articles that appeared in *The New York Times* on July 1998, Posada Carriles said that Jorge Mas Canosa had given him $200,000 for his operations. This defamatory and false claim sought to undermine the Foundation's cornerstone pledge: to seek freedom and human rights for Cuba, but only to do so through peaceful means. The publication was very alarming to the Foundation's directors. Although Jorge Mas Canosa had passed away by then, his wife Irma asked me to do whatever I could to make the newspaper issue a retraction.

We immediately submitted a forceful denial, which the nice guys at *The New York Times* printed on page seven with the title: "Cuban Exiles Say *Times* Articles are Baseless." The story was dwarfed by a near-full-page CitiBank ad: "Pay Two Bills On-Line, Get $25." As usual, *The New York Times* was determined to criticize and defame the Cuban American exile community, while giving hardly any space for us to defend ourselves and tell the truth.

They underestimated our ability to wage a counterattack. We obtained every *New York Times* article, editorial, and op-ed written about the Foundation going back to 1989. Every mention of the Foundation was negative and disparaging. Ninoska Peréz went on radio and TV to assert that the allegations in *The New York Times* articles were false. We then scheduled a series of press conferences in different cities, including Miami and Washington, D.C.

On July 16, 1998, the Foundation hosted a press conference in Washington, D.C., in the First Amendment Room of the National Press Club. We denounced *The New York Times* articles and demanded a retraction. We also announced that we were filing a lawsuit against the newspaper for publishing defamatory and malicious allegations.

Luis Posada Carriles soon gave an on-camera interview denying *The New York Times'* claims. On July 13, 1998, he met with Rafael Orizondo, a reporter of Miami's Channel 23, at undisclosed location. The interview was conducted clandestinely because Posada Carriles felt he was in danger of being assassinated or kidnapped. He adamantly denied that he said the Foundation members financed any of his activities, and he charged that *The New York Times* reporters had "manipulated" his comments.

In a *Sun Sentinel* article on July 14, 1998, Posada Carriles was reported as saying, "I have never received any money from the foundation or Mas Canosa or any of its officials. . . . Never. I'm an independent man. I don't represent anyone. I don't know why those reporters said that."

Once we exposed the weak underpinnings of *The New York Times* article, other newspapers realized that the *Times* had failed to properly vet the story. On July 17, 1998, the *Sun Sentinel* published an article called "Exile Group to Sue *Times*, Claiming Libel in Stories," which stated the following:

Keith Woods, a journalism ethics professor at the Poynter Institute for Media Studies in St. Petersburg, said he thinks the Cuban American National Foundation has a legitimate complaint with a series published earlier this week.

Woods stated as follows: "This story made fairly hot indictments of the Foundation and Mas mostly based on an interview with someone whose credibility should have been questioned, and that was going out on a limb. The story asked readers to accept a great deal of information purely on faith."

Woods was a former editor of the *New Orleans Times Picayune*. I did not influence his opinion in any way. He went on the say the following:

Beyond Posada, I don't read much backing up of what's there. One has to assume the paper has more facts than they have provided the readers. Overall, I think the story is light on attribution, considering the current journalism environment we are in.

The story may have been falling apart, but Fidel Castro was ecstatic anyways. As usual, *The New York Times* had managed to please the dictator. On July 26, 1998, one of Castro's days of celebration (the fortieth anniversary of a battle fought in support of his so-called revolution), Castro gave a speech where he went on and on about *The New York Times* article. He claimed it was proof that the Foundation had made attempts on his life. He began his speech with the following:

What does *The New York Times* say about one of the most well-known anti-revolutionary terrorists based in the United States? [and then he lied] and I will also limit to that which is essential, I look at my watch, know that it is hot, but perhaps this material may be of interest.

Castro went on to say:

Posada expressed that his bombings had been supported by the leaders of the Foundation and its founder and head, Jorge Mas Canosa, who died last year, and had been well received in the White House by Presidents Reagan, Bush, and Clinton.

He was a powerful force in the Florida elections, not only in the national ones but also in the state elections, and was a well-known political contributor to these campaigns. Mas Canosa played a decisive role in persuading Clinton to change his way of thinking and to continue imposing sanctions and isolating Castro's Cuba.

Then he proceeded to read *The New York Times* article word for word.

Castro wasn't speaking to the Cuban people—who care very little about *The New York Times*—he was speaking to us. Ultimately, he shifted the blame for all of Posada's activities directly onto the real object of his hatred: the United States of America. "[Posada] realized these operations without the complicity, tolerance, and support of the American authorities," Castro said, alluding to Posada Carriles' terrorist activities. But to ensure that he didn't go too far and make Bill Clinton angry—he said the following:

But I want to be frank; I want to be clear; I do not want to make accusations. We do not blame the present administration for these acts; we do not believe that Mr. Clinton is capable of ordering attempts against political leaders and terrorist plans against another country. Such an accusation does not reconcile with the idea, with the concept, with the information that we have about him. Really, if I believe that, I would say so here.

Castro theorized that the Foundation had duped the innocent Mr. Clinton. He exaggerated the Foundation's political power, claiming that we owned all of Miami's radio and TV stations and controlled the jobs at Miami City Hall. In an incoherent ramble, Castro claimed that Cuban Americans were colonialists who received better treatment in the United States than other Latin American immigrant groups.

Castro then turned his attention to the Foundation's threat to sue *The New York Times*. He recommended that the paper not issue a retraction, arguing that any self-respecting newspaper should refuse to be discredited.

Near the end of his speech, Castro disclosed his great fear that the Foundation could arrest him if he travelled outside Cuba. He was aware that we organized "hunts" against him whenever he took international trips. He claimed that he would not stop traveling, however, and emphatically stated that he was unafraid. To me, he meant (as usual) just the opposite: he was afraid. He stopped traveling, after all.

Castro claimed that when he visited Salvador Allende, the socialist former president of Chile, he was followed throughout the country by pseudo-newspapermen carrying Venezuelan passports "with Venezuelan television cameras that had automatic weapons inside the television projectors, and they were at press interviews but a few paces before me." He continued:

What happened to them? They weren't fanatics. They

did not dare to fire, because they knew they would die also, and mercenaries don't die. What mercenaries want is money, and the enemies of the revolution have been fundamentally mercenaries who want to live to enjoy the money they'd get for killing me.

I have no idea where Castro got the notion that there were automatic weapons inside the TV cameras, but it does highlight his paranoia and precarious mental condition.

Back in the U.S., *The New York Times* refused to provide a retraction, claiming that the two authors had a recording of the interview. We already had a tape of Posada Carriles denying that he gave the defamatory statement to Ann Louise Bardach; I therefore demanded that *The New York Times* produce their tape of the original interview and prove their allegations. It was never produced. If the tape actually existed, it would have been simple for them to clear up the issue, but they never did.

Moreover, our investigation indicated that perhaps there weren't two New York Times reporters present in the interview; but only one: Ann Louise Bardach. That left *The New York Times* standing on only one leg—and a particularly wobbly one at that. Bardach had a proven track record of hostility towards the Foundation. The *Times* apparently was unaware that Bardach had written the article for the New Republic that called Jorge Mas Canosa a mobster and the New Republic had settled. Our sources told us that there was an emotional confrontation between Bardach and the *Times* once they learned about the *New Republic* article.

No tape, no second writer—and a writer hostile to her subject who had previously written an article unsupported by the facts. Still, *The New York Times* refused to retract the story.

I arranged a meeting with *The New York Times* editorial board on July 22, 1998, at their offices. Jorge Mas Santos, Pepe

Hernández, Alberto Hernández, and myself were all in attendance. In all my life, I have never met more arrogant people than
those at the *Times*. The meeting quickly turned into a screaming
match. I was able to explain the weakness of their case in detail
and told them we would file a lawsuit if the article wasn't retract-
ed. They seemed surprised by our evidence, but continued to act
defiant and hostile.

The lawyer for *The New York Times*, Adam Liptak, told me
that his newspaper had never lost a defamation suit. I told him
to brace himself—I intended to file the lawsuit in Miami and
could easily predict that we'd win a jury verdict. I jokingly
warned him that the case would be decided by Pepe, Juan,
Roberto, and Pedro.

I left the meeting with a better understanding of why *The
New York Times* is so pro-Castro and anti-Cuban American in
their articles and editorials. The reason is simple: they hate
Cuban Americans. Their distaste for us was palpably obvious in
the meeting. I tried to keep it civil when I explained to them why
a retraction was needed; as a lawyer, I always try to keep discussions professional. But the battle quickly became personal for
them—even more so than it was for us!

We left the meeting without getting a retraction, but I
agreed to keep talking with Liptak, who was competent and professional. My legal position was sound, and I wanted to give *The
New York Times* editorial board something to think about, so I
wrote the following letter to *Times* publisher Arthur Ochs
Sulzberger, Jr. and Joseph Lelyveld, Executive Editor:

"It is clear that your writers, in their zeal to destroy the
image of the Foundation and otherwise advance their
own political agenda, broke basic rules of sound journalism and proceeded to publish statements knowing that
they were false and in reckless disregard for the truth,

with ill will, hostility, and an intent to cause harm. As you know, recklessness may be found where there are obvious reasons, such as in this case, to doubt the veracity of the informant or the accuracy of his reports.

"The aforementioned articles themselves show, beyond doubt, that the one and only source of these allegations is a person who works covertly, is a master at deception, and makes frequent contradictory statements. A newspaper with the influence of *The New York Times* should proceed with caution and particular care to ensure that its sources are sound so that what occurred, i.e., a full denial by the source of the statements within a day of the article published, does not occur.

The New York Times should have done a more thorough investigation of the facts alleged. For example, a cursory investigation of prior news reports and stories relative to Mr. Posada Carriles would have confirmed that he had denied any involvement by the Foundation or its leaders in his activities. Furthermore, there was no need to rush this story without a full investigation. When an article is not in the category of 'hot news,' that is, information that must be printed immediately or it will lose its newsworthy value, actual malice may be inferred when the investigation for a story is grossly inadequate in the circumstances."

Once *The New York Times* received the letter, Liptak wrote me the following response:

We are confused by your assertion that an earlier lawsuit against Ann Louise Bardach by Jorge Mas Canosa and the Foundation is evidence of bias by Ms. Bardach. Put aside, that Ms. Bardach was dismissed from the lawsuit and that the

New Republic settlement concerned solely a headline for which she was not responsible. Your suggestion seems to be that the mere filing of a lawsuit is sufficient to forbid any reporter named as a defendant from ever reporting on the plaintiff again.

By this time, Posada Carriles had repeatedly denied making the accusations or deliberately providing misleading information to *The New York Times*. What follows is a portion of a translated transcript of María Elvira Salazar's CBS interview with Luis Posada Carriles, which aired on August 2, 1998. Salazar is an icon of Cuban American political news, and everybody in Miami was glued to her station:

MES: Look, Posada, for decades you did not grant interviews to the press. Why did you grant that first interview regarding your activities, your life, and about what you're doing to *The New York Times*?

LPC: *The New York Times* reporter made contact with me through a Venezuelan friend, Ernesto, the husband of fashion designer Carolina Herrera. I accepted to speak with her via telephone. She explained—she told me, literally—that she wanted to do an article to clarify many negative things that were coming out in the American papers against us. She said that I had raised the image of those who struggle for freedom and that she wanted to do a favorable interview about me and my cause, above all else. I wasn't interested in talking about myself, but the cause did interest me. And that she was going to help us. Let me explain something that I believe [unintelligible]. She doesn't speak Spanish, nothing. My English is deficient. That was why we had so many communication problems. And it may be that she interpreted many of the things that I said erroneously or did so maliciously.

MES: Let's talk a bit, then, about how you said that she could have misinterpreted some of the things that you said. Let's go point-by-point: there are two or three, four very important points in those two articles in *The New York Times* that I would like you to clarify. *The New York Times* says one thing; the Cuban American National Foundation says another; a local Miami station obtained an interview with you a few hours later in which you said another. Then, please clarify. The first *New York Times* article says that the bombings and the assassination attempts were financially supported by members of the CANF. That is one of the affirmations in that piece. Did you say that or not?

LPC: Completely false. I am responding to your question categorically. If the Cuban American National Foundation financed undercover operations in Cuba, operations [unintelligible], that is completely false. I have not said that.

As we can see, Posada Carriles strongly denied *The New York Times'* version of the events. I continued to demand a recording of the original *Times* interview between Posada Carriles and Bardach, but no one ever gave it to me. From a purely legal and logical standpoint, *The New York Times* had no choice but to issue a retraction.

There was one more development that may have tipped the scales. Adam Liptak contacted Jack Weiss, now Dean of the Louisiana State University Law School. Weiss was once editor-in-chief of the *Harvard Law Review* and is known nationally as a brilliant lawyer and one of the foremost First Amendment experts in the country. We were partners at my prior law firm and are friends of many years. We had worked together on cases. Jack called to let me know about their discussion. He told Liptak that, given the circumstances of the case, a verdict in favor of the Foundation was all but certain if *The New York Times* was sued in Miami.

After our meeting-turned-shouting-match, Liptak and I struggled to agree on the terms of what I called a retraction and what he called an "editors' note." Liptak wrote me the following:

The *Times* has on many occasions publicly stated that editors' notes amplify articles or rectify what the editors consider significant lapses of fairness, balance, or perspective.

We were headed in the right direction.

Liptak recognized that they were under great pressure; other newspapers would relish the opportunity to take a shot at the arrogant *New York Times*. Ultimately, the editorial board relented, and the newspaper issued an editors' note.

We at the Foundation immediately got to work spinning the story. The South Florida newspapers helped transform the story of our "editors' note" into a major victory over the country's most powerful newspaper. On July 14, the *Miami Herald* published an article with the headline: "Exile Denies CANF Leaders Financed Attacks in Cuba," and subtitle: "Luis Posada Carriles said he had never received any money from Mas Canosa." The Foundation hosted standing-room-only press conferences that detailed the basis of the lawsuit against *The New York Times*. The Mas family, a force to be reckoned with in Miami, attended these conferences.

The New York Times editors' note confirmed the misleading nature of the story and ultimately made the newspaper look very foolish. Other newspapers hailed the outcome as a great victory for the Foundation. To be honest, the note was somewhat of a weak, negotiated deal, but I knew that any retraction made after such a well-publicized fight would be viewed as a significant defeat for the paper.

After seeing that the story had appeared nationally, Liptak admitted to me that the Foundation had done quite a job spinning the story. I told him that we had no choice since the pro-Castro media was opposed to conservative Cuban Americans.

We had learned to fight back.

THE CIVIL CASE OF THE BROTHERS TO THE RESCUE SHOOTDOWN

ON FEBRUARY 24, 1996, CASTRO MURDERED THREE AMERICAN citizens and one permanent resident over the Florida Straits. The victims were piloting two unarmed civilian planes as they searched for rafters in the waters between Cuba and the Florida Keys. The deceased were all members of Brothers to the Rescue—an organization dedicated to helping Cuban emigrants and ending Castro's regime through nonviolent methods. The group rescued thousands of Cuban rafters in the 1990s.

Castro carried out this murder with the help Los Cinco, also known as the Cuban Five. These five Cuban spies were later convicted by Guy Lewis, then-U.S. Attorney for the Southern District of Florida, and are currently serving time in U.S. prisons.

The Brothers to the Rescue mission that day was to locate rafters and provide them with life-saving assistance by informing the U.S. Coast Guard of their location. Three planes took off on the morning of February 24, 1996, but only one would return. The founder of Brothers to the Rescue, José Basulto, flew in the first plane with his passenger, Silvia Iriondo. Carlos Alberto Costa piloted the second plane; his copilot was Pablo Morales, a Cuban national who had once been a rafter. Mario M. de la Peña piloted the second plane with Armando Alejandre as his passenger.

Before departing, the planes notified both Miami and Havana traffic controllers of their flight plan, which would take them south of the twenty-fourth parallel—far north of Cuba's twelve-mile territorial sea.

While the two planes were still north of the twenty-fourth parallel, the Cuban Air Force launched two military aircraft, a MiG-29 and a MiG-23 operating under the control of Cuba's military ground station. The MiGs carried guns, close-range missiles, bombs, and rockets. The Cuban Air Force pilots were trained and experienced in combat.

Excerpts from the radio communications between the MiG-29 and Havana Military Control were later presented at trial:

MiG-29	OK, the target is in sight; the target is in sight. It's a small aircraft. Copied, small aircraft in sight.
MiG-29	OK, we have it in sight, we have it in sight.
MiG-29	The target is in sight.
Military Control	Go ahead.
MiG-29	The target is in sight.
Military Control	Aircraft in sight.
MiG-29	Come again?
MiG-29	It's a small aircraft, a small aircraft.
MiG-29	It's white, white.
Military Control	Color and registration of the aircraft?

Military Control	Buddy.
MiG-29	Listen, the registration also?
Military Control	What kind and color?
MiG-29	It is white and blue.
MiG-29	White and blue, at a low altitude, a small aircraft.
MiG-29	Give me instructions.
MiG-29	Instructions!
MiG-29	Listen, authorize me . . .
MiG-29	If we give it a pass, it will complicate things. We are going to give it a pass. Because some vessels are approaching there, I am going to give it a pass.
MiG-29	Talk, talk.
MiG-29	I have it in lock-on. I have it in lock-on.
MiG-29	We have it in lock-on. Give us authorization.
MiG-29	It is a Cessna 337. That one. Give us authorization, damn it!
Military Control	Fire.
MiG-29	Give us authorization damn it, we have it.
Military Control	Authorized to destroy.
MiG-29	I'm going to pass it.

Military Control	Authorized to destroy.
MiG-29	We already copied. We already copied.
Military Control	Authorized to destroy.
MiG-29	Understood, already received. Already received. Leave us alone for now.
Military Control	Don't lose it.
MiG-29	First launch.
MiG-29	We hit him! Damn! We hit him! We hit him! We retired him!
MiG-29	Wait to see where it fell.
MiG-29	Come on in, come on in! Damn, we hit.
MiG-29	Mark the place where we took it out.
MiG-29	We are over it. This one won't mess around anymore.
Military Control	Congratulations to the two of you.
MiG-29	Mark the spot.
MiG-29	We're climbing and returning home.
Military Control	Stand by there circling above.
MiG-29	Over the target
Military	Correct.

Control

MiG-29   S—t, we did tell you, Buddy.

Military   Correct, the target is marked.
Control

MiG-29   Go ahead.

Military   OK, climb to 3,200, 4,000 meters above the
Control   destroyed target and maintain economical speed.

MiG-29   Go ahead.

Military   I need you to stand by . . . there. What heading
Control   did the launch have?

MiG-29   I have another aircraft in sight.

MiG-29   We have another aircraft.

Military   Follow it. Don't lose the other small aircraft.
Control

MiG-29   We have another aircraft in sight. It's in the area
          where [the first aircraft] fell. It's in the area where
          it fell.

MiG-29   We have the aircraft in sight.

Military   Stand by.
Control
MiG-29   Comrade. It's in the area of the event.

MiG-29   Did you copy?

MiG-29   OK, this aircraft is headed 90 degrees now.

MiG-29   It's in the area of the event, where the target fell.
          They're going to have to authorize us.

MiG-29	Hey, the SAR isn't needed. Nothing remains, nothing.
Military Control	Correct, keep following the aircraft. You're going to stay above above it.
MiG-29	We're above it.
Military Control	Correct . . .
MiG-29	For what?
MiG-29	Is the other authorized?
Military Control	Correct.
MiG-29	Great. Let's go Alberto.
MiG-29	Understood; we are now going to destroy it.
Military Control	Do you still have it in sight?
MiG-29	We have it, we have it, we're working. Let us work.
MiG-29	The other is destroyed, the other is destroyed. Fatherland or death, s—t! The other is down also.

The recording gives ample evidence of the inhumanity of this act. The pilots were elated by their cowardly attack. Their behavior was consistent with the example set by Castro, who never hesitated to hurt or kill those who were defenseless. Despite being educated at the Jesuit School in Belen, Castro is a godless, cruel, and vicious man. It is hard to believe that pilots operating armed MiGs could get joy out of killing men in tiny unarmed planes. But the radio transmission is proof that they did.

In books written by Cuban political prisoners, such as *Against All Hope*[17] by Armando Valladares, there are countless stories of ecstatic abuse by Castro's men. Before entering the cells, guards would work themselves into a trancelike rage so that they could enjoy inflicting pain on their defenseless captives. I've given away many copies of Armando Valladares's book to those who cannot believe the cruelty that Castro expected and rewarded.

The families of the murdered Brothers to the Rescue pilots filed a civil complaint. Among them were Marlena Alejandre, on behalf of Armando Alejandre; Mirta Mendez, on behalf of Carlos Alberto Costa; and Mario and Miriam de la Peña on behalf of Mario M. de la Peña. Pablo Morales' family was not part of this civil action.

A trial was held before Judge James Lawrence King of the Southern District of Florida. The case was brought by—among others—Frank Angones, Ronald Kleinman, Bob Martinez, Aaron Podhurst, and Victor Diaz. Frank was a good friend of one of the murdered pilots, Armando Alejandre.

In a thirty-three page opinion given on December 17, 1997, Judge King entered a judgment against the government of Cuba and the Cuban Air Force in the amount of $187,627,911.00 for compensatory and punitive damages. In his moving and powerfully worded decision, Judge King found as follows:

The Cuban Air Force never notified or warned the civilian planes, never attempted other methods of interception, and never gave them the opportunity to land. The MiGs first and only response was the intentional and malicious destruction of the Brothers to the Rescue planes and their four innocent occupants. . . .

Cuba's extrajudicial killings of Mario T. de la Peña,

---

[17]Armando Valladares, Against All Hope (Encounter Books, 2001).

Carlos Alberto Costa, and Armando Alejandre violated clearly established principles of international law. More importantly, they were inhumane acts against innocent civilians. The fact that the killings were premeditated and intentional, outside of Cuban territory, wholly disproportionate, and executed without warning or process makes this act unique in its brazen flouting of international norms. There appears to be no precedent for a military aircraft intentionally shooting down an unarmed, civilian plane.

José Basulto showed me the plane that survived. To me, it was so small it looked like a toy. Jose offered to give me a ride, but I declined because the cabin was so tiny it made me feel claustrophobic. The men who Castro assassinated were true men of courage. Although he did not have to, Judge King honored each of them individually. He wrote the following about Armando Alejandre:

Armando Alejandre was forty-five years old at the time of his murder. Alejandre, although born in Cuba, served an active tour of duty for eight months in Vietnam, completed his college education at Florida International University, and worked as a consultant to the Metro-Dade Transit Authority at the time of his death. He was survived by his wife of twenty-one years, Marlene, and his daughter, Marlene, a college student.

Carlos Alberto Acosta was "only twenty-nine years old when the Cuban government ended his life." Judge King noted his interest in aviation and his hope to someday oversee the operations of a major airport. Acosta earned his Bachelor's Degree at Embry-Riddle Aeronautical University and worked as a training specialist for the Dade County Aviation Department. He was survived by his parents and his sister.

Mario Manuel de la Peña was also born in the United States and was but twenty-four years old at the time of his murder. His goal was to become an airline pilot, and he was in his last semester at Embry-Riddle when he was killed. During that semester, he had obtained a "coveted and highly competitive internship with American Airlines." Embry-Riddle posthumously granted him a Bachelor's Degree in Professional Aeronautics. He was survived by his younger brother, Michael, and his parents, Mario T. de la Peña and Miriam de la Peña.

It is hard for me to write about these patriots without becoming emotional. It is just that I have seen so much pain inflicted by Castro and his cohorts go unpunished.

Havana Yacht Club

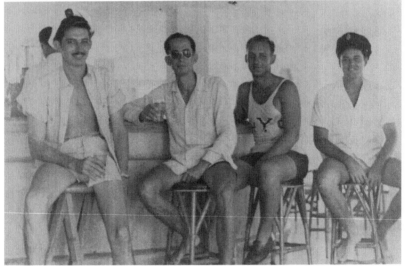

Pictured far left: my Father

Pictured second from the left: George Fowler, my Father

Havana Yacht Club Party, January 1955

Eduardo and Mercedes Jenkins, wedding of my wife's parents in Varadero Beach

Pictured center: Eduardo Jenkins, my Father-in-law and the team coach

In the center, Cristina's mom, Mercedes Jenkins, and her Father, Eduardo Jenkins, at the Kawama Club in Vardero Beach pre-Castro

My Wife, Cristina (far left) with Sisters, Vicky and Mercedes (Carmen is not in picture). Taken before their mother was forced to send them out of Cuba alone and place them in foster care with the assistance of the CIA Peter Pan Program

Article.
On January 11,
1959, Castro strips
the population of
their weapons

Camla Dictionary · **The Miami Herald** · Section B
Tuesday, December 25, 1962 · Complete State News

The Merriest Christmas For the Alberto Fowlers

By PAT MANGAN
Of Our Broward Bureau

FORT LAUDERDALE — It's the merriest of Christmases at 1501 SW Fourth Ct., where a son is home from a Cuban prison.

Alberto Fowler, 33, lighter, calloused from sleeping on the bare floor, and willing to do without rice and macaroni for the rest of his life, is having a happy Christmas.

So are his father, George, his wife, Paulette, and four-year-old Alberto Jr., who showered his father with hundreds of kisses on the way home from Miami Sunday night.

Alberto's two - year - old daughter, Alexandra, with her grandmother in New Orleans, hasn't seen her father yet.

The scene at the Fowlers on Christmas Eve was one of exultant confusion.

"For two years I've planned the meal for Alberto and the flowers for the house," said his stepmother, Mrs. George Fowler. "Now look, we're eating hamburgers."

Nobody cared.

Alberto and Guido Conti, 1515 Seabreeze Ave., spent part of their time in prison filling a 200-page book with menus of the meals they'd like to have.

They were told they would die if Cuba was invaded.

Alberto said the prisoners kept up their morale by maintaining strict military discipline among themselves. When they were told they were going

home, no one showed a reaction.

They didn't want the guards to know how they felt, nor the other political prisoners who wouldn't be released.

During the Russian missile crisis, the prisoners' guards discussed their resentment of Castro being bossed by the Russians, Alberto said, and took out their ill feeling on the prisoners.

What's next for him?

"I'm going to rest, but I remain at the orders of the revolutionary government," he said.

It's a Joyous Christmas -- Daddy's Home
... Cuban prisoner Alberto Fowler, wife and son
—Herald Photo by MEL KENYON

Tio Alberto, his wife Paulette, and his son Chico after he was released
from prison following his capture during the Bay of Pigs, *Miami Herald*,
December 25, 1962

Havana, September 24, 2012, the Ladies in White gathered for the day of Our Lady of Mercy, patron saint of men in captivity. Planning to make a peaceful walk to the Patron's church in Old Havana, their purpose was to implore that the Patron invest her efforts, her holy hands, and her love in the hearts of the island's government officials so that there could be an end to the violence, injustice and cruelty these men have imposed on the Cuban people. Agents of the National Security, ordered by the government, stood at the home in which the women gathered (Neptune St. #963) and used force to push, maltreat, and beat the women back into the house, repressing the women from their right to walk to the church and pray.

Alejandra Garcia de la Riva and Dolia Leal Francisco, Ladies in White, forcefully taken by the police during peceful demonstration on April 21, 2008, at the Plaza José Marti

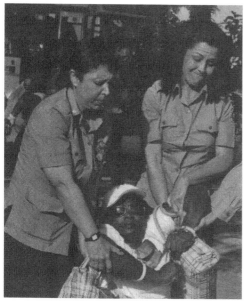

Marta Fonseca, Lady in White, violently suppressed with karate techniques during a peaceful demonstration on March 17, 2010

Berta Soler, the leader of the Ladies in White, violently detained by Cuban Police at the Plaza Jose Martí on April 21, 2008

The lady holding her hat is Berta Soler. Berta Soler told me she was being beaten and held up by Castro's mob

Cristina Fowler arrived in the United States as a child after the Cuban revolution. Her parents, who came two years later with only the clothes on their backs, worked to send five children to college

Lech Walesa, Liberator of Poland and me

Laly Sampedro (CANF) and Yoani Sanchez (The Brave Blogger)

My family and friends during anti-Castro rallies in New Orleans and me

Senator Connie Mack, Jorge Mas Canosa, Senator Robert Torricelli, and Jeb Bush at CANF rally

Jorge Mas Canosa and Jesse Jackson

Jorge Mas Canosa and the Iron Lady

Me, Cristina and Mayor Giuliani in Lafayette, LA

Senator David Vitter, Me, and President George H. W. Bush

Jorge Mas Santos, Senator Joe Liberman, Senator Bill Nelson, and Me at CANF Embassy in Washington, DC

Guillermo Farinas and Me in CANF offices

Senator John McCain, me and
Governor Bobby Jindal of Louisiana

Jorge Mas Canosa and
Ronald Reagan

Jorge Mas Canosa and Bill Clinton

Jorge Mas Canosa and Senator Bob
Torricelli at the Orange Bowl

Berta Soler and Clara
Maria del Valle with
Pope Francis

Pope Benedict and
Clara Maria del Valle
asking for help in
Cuba

Cristina, Alberto de
Jongh, Lieutenant
Governor of
Louisiana
Jay Dardenne,
Omar Lopez
Montenegro and me

THE ARGUMENT FOR CASTRO'S INDICTMENT

JUDGE KING'S DECISION GIVES THE U.S. GOVERNMENT AMPLE evidence for a prosecution against Castro for murder. According to Judge King, the first plane was eighteen miles from the Cuban coast when it was shot down, while the second one was 30.5 miles away. These numbers placed the planes well outside the twelve-mile territorial sea claimed by Cuba and permitted under international law. Noting that the plaintiffs and three of the four murdered pilots were U.S. citizens, the court had no problem finding U.S. jurisdiction for this case.

I prepared an opinion asking for the indictment of Castro and gave it to Tom Scott and Guy Lewis, two successive U.S. Attorneys for the Southern District of Florida. Jorge Mas Canosa, Pepe Hernández and I met with Tom Scott. Both Tom and Guy wanted to indict Castro, but our government wouldn't let them. Since then, Guy has repeatedly urged the indictment.

My legal memorandum notes that in the March 11, 1996 edition of Time Magazine, Fidel Castro admitted to approving the directive to stop the Brothers to the Rescue planes—by any means necessary—if they appeared to be trespassing into Cuban airspace. The Time interviewer specifically asked Fidel about the chain of command with respect to the directive. Castro replied:

We discussed it with Raúl [Castro's brother and head of the defense forces] and the Joint Chiefs of Staff. We agreed that planes dropping leaflets on Havana cannot happen again. We gave the order to the head of the Air Force. On Saturday [February 24, 1996], the Brothers planes came twice. The San Antonio Air Base was on high alert. On the third pass, they scrambled and did their job. They shot the planes down. They are professionals. They did what they believe is the right thing. These are all people we trust, but I take responsibility for what happened.

It so happened that this attack occurred after a weeklong wave of repression by the Cuban government against Concilio Cubano, a Cuban umbrella organization of human rights activists, dissidents, independent economists, and journalists. This included arrests, strip-searches, house arrests, and—in some cases—multi-year jail sentences. The shootdown was Castro's warning to the people of Cuba that he was capable of anything— even killing unarmed U.S. citizens in international waters. He wanted to show that he did not fear the United States.

Legally, I asked for the application of 18 U.S.C. ¶ 2332 et. seq., which renders as a federal criminal offense the murder or conspiracy to murder a U.S. national while that national is outside the United States.[18]

---

[18]In pertinent part, the statute provides that

a) Homicide. Whoever kills a national of the United States, while such national is outside the United States, shall (1) if the killing is murder, as defined in §1111(a), be fined under this title punished by death or imprisonment for any term of years to life, or both; and (2) if the killing is voluntary manslaughter as defined in §1112(a) of this title, be fined under this title or imprisoned for not less than ten years or both.

* * *

b) Attempt or conspiracy with regard to homicide. Whoever outside the United States attempts to kill, or engages in a conspiracy to kill, a national of the United States shall

18 U.S.C. §1111(a) defines murder as the "unlawful killing of a human being with malice or forethought." I also believe that 18 U.S.C. §2332(b) was applicable, which criminalizes acts of terrorism transcending national boundaries.[19]

The Terrorist Section describes acts of terrorism transcending national boundaries. This meant that even if a judge ruled that the shootdown occurred within the U.S. territorial waters and 18 U.S.C. §2332 did not apply, there was an alternative cause of action under the Terrorism Statute. Accordingly, I concluded that regardless of the status of the shootdown, Fidel Castro could be indicted under federal law.

In our efforts to indict Castro, we needed to keep in mind an important procedural consideration—the statutory certification requirement. In particular, 18 U.S.C. §2332 (d) requires that before prosecuting an individual under the statute, the U.S. attorney must obtain prior certification by the Attorney General that the offense was intended to coerce, intimidate or retaliate against the government or a civilian population. We had to check whether this requirement was satisfied in the Brothers to the Rescue case.

---

* * *

(2) in the case of a conspiracy ... to commit a killing that is a murder as defined in section 1111(a) of this title, if one or more of such persons do any overt act to effect the completion of the conspiracy, be fined under this title or imprisoned for any term of years or for life, or both so fined and so imprisoned.

[19] In particular, this statute provides that:

(a) Prohibited acts

(1) Offenses-whoever involving conduct transcending national boundaries and in a circumstance described in subsection (b)

(a) kills ... any person within the United States; in violation of the laws of any state, the United States, shall be punished by death or by imprisonment for any term of years or life.

Fortunately, the Foundation had already taken care of it. This statutory certification requirement was satisfied in the Cuban Liberty and Democratic Solidarity (LIBERTAD) Act of 1996, where the U.S. Congress made a specific legislative finding that the attack was timed in order to intimidate and retaliate against the Concilio Cubano. The finding was supported by the fact that Brothers to the Rescue had flown its humanitarian missions for several years "prior to the attack."

There was another problem: Since Castro was a head of state, he had immunity under either federal statute. I dealt with that legal issue by alluding to the case of *Jimenez v. Aristeguieta*[20]. In 1962, the Fifth Circuit Court of Appeals rejected the claims of Marcos Pérez Jiménez—a former Venezuelan dictator—that his criminal acts were acts of state that precluded prosecution. In that case, the Fifth Circuit concluded that the dictator's actions were for his own benefit and could not be characterized as sovereign acts; therefore, they were not entitled state protection.

The memorandum argued that the radio communications between the MiG-29 and the Havana Military Control indicated that they had affirmatively identified the Brothers to the Rescue planes as civilian aircraft. It was equally clear that the plane was neither inside nor flying toward Cuban airspace. Therefore, the shootdown was an ultra vires act, without provocation and wholly unrelated to any sovereign right to preserve Cuban national security.

The head of state defense does not apply when the acts underlying the criminal indictment are not "authorized official acts." For example, when the U.S. indicted the Panamanian dictator Manuel Noriega, his drug-related activities were not considered to be acts of state because they had only furthered his own self-interest.

By shooting down planes manned by his political opponents,

---

[20] Jimenez v. Aristeguieta, 311 F.2d 547, 557-58 (5th Cir. 1962).

Castro had committed an extra-governmental act. Therefore, our criminal indictment should have been unfettered by any claim to head of state immunity. In short, if you kill people only to further your own best interest—i.e., to stay in control as dictator—you do not enjoy head of state immunity.

Head of state immunity is designed to protect international comity and respect by allowing leaders to perform governmental duties without fear of prosecution by foreign courts. But it was never designed to insulate those who seize power by force from the consequences of their actions. Common sense dictates that those who commit crimes while purporting to be a head of state should not be protected.

Simultaneously with my efforts to obtain a federal criminal indictment, I sought the indictment of Castro under Florida state law. I presented my case personally to Governor Jeb Bush; Bob Butterworth, the Attorney General of Florida; and Katherine Fernandez Rundle, the City Attorney. I met with each of them separately and urged them to indict Castro. All were sympathetic, but no indictment came.

In Florida, a "principal of the first degree" is defined as anyone who "aids, abets, counsels, hires, or otherwise procures any criminal offense against the state to be committed and such offense is committed or is attempted to be committed." Also in Florida, murder (defined simply as "the unlawful killing of a human being") in the first degree requires "a premeditated design to affect the death of . . . any human being."[21]

I argued that Castro acted as a principal in a conspiracy to commit first-degree murder. Fidel Castro himself was never physically present in Florida at any time during the planning or implementation of the shootdown; however, Florida does have criminal jurisdiction to prosecute Fidel Castro for conspiring to commit first-degree murder. Under Florida Statute 910.005, a

[21] Florida Statute §782.04 (1)(a)(1).

person is subject to prosecution in Florida for an offense that he commits—while either within or outside the state—by her or his own conduct or that of another for which the person is legally accountable. The statue applies if "the conduct within the state constitutes an attempt or conspiracy to commit in another jurisdiction an offense under the laws of both [Florida] and the other jurisdiction."

The Florida Supreme Court has concluded that they can prosecute a murder committed on the high seas so long as an essential element of the crime occurred within the state and there is at least concurrent jurisdiction with the federal government. In this case, Fidel Castro had spies covertly operating in Miami who prepared the events for the shootdown.

Since our initial attempts, we have given this same legal memorandum to President Clinton, President Bush, and Governor Jeb Bush. The evidence of Castro's guilt is incontrovertible, but our nation's most powerful politicians have yet to act.

In a rather controversial fashion, I personally ensured the memorandum's delivery to then-U.S. Attorney General John Ashcroft. In June 2001, Ashcroft was scheduled to visit the Versailles Restaurant in Miami's Little Havana to meet with a group of Cuban exiles who were opposed to the Foundation. Because I was General Counsel of the Foundation, I was prevented from visiting with him. Fortunately, one of our directors, Felipe Valls—owner of the Versailles Restaurant and a veritable icon in the Cuban American community—snuck me inside.

I was there alone when Ashcroft appeared. He took a liking to me, and we had a lengthy conversation about my efforts to indict Castro. He seemed largely ignorant of the issue. Eventually, his Cuban handlers told the FBI that I had not been invited, and I was asked to leave three times. When it looked like I was about to be arrested, I stepped outside to address the many reporters waiting outside. The news media knew me and what

my intention was, and they were surprised that I had been ejected. MSNBC reported my comments: "We know who gave the
order, because he admitted it. So we don't have to wait any
longer. I think John Ashcroft has to indict Fidel Castro for the
murder of the Brothers to the Rescue pilots."

After I was kicked out, the Attorney General had lunch with
several Cuban exiles. José Basulto was allowed into the meeting,
accompanied by the mother of one of the murdered pilots. He
presented Ashcroft with the legal memo that I had prepared.

Ashcroft's meeting with the Cuban exiles was described in
the papers as fruitful but noncommittal on the indictment issue.
No television cameras were allowed inside the restaurant.
Ashcroft's publicity trip to Little Havana was a flop; he was simply unprepared for the pressure to indict Castro. I guess he
thought he could earn our goodwill just by enjoying a plate of
pork and plantains.

The Brothers to the Rescue murders was Castro's biggest
mistake, but our country has yet to act on it. Justice has been
denied. A successful indictment would weaken Castro both
internationally and in Cuba. I would love for us to pick him up
like Saddam Hussein or Manuel Noriega. Although I doubt that
our politics will ever allow it, it is exactly what justice deserves.

THE MOCK TRIAL OF CASTRO FOR THE BROTHERS TO THE RESCUE MURDERS

CASTRO MADE A MAJOR MISTAKE WHEN HE ORDERED THE shootdown. Because his MiG fighters violated U.S. jurisdiction and his spies were caught plotting within U.S. borders, the action subjected him to prosecution in the United States.

I prepared a mock trial of Castro for the murder of the Brothers to the Rescue pilots. On July 15, 1999, I presented the trial before the Sub-Committee on Crime of the Committee of the Judiciary of the House of Representatives. Congressman Bill McCollum, a strong ally of our cause, hosted the event.

I gave the following statement to the House of Representatives:

> Thank you, Mr. McCollum. I came to this country forty years ago at the age of nine as a refugee from Cuba, so I am very honored and in awe of being here before this committee. I thank you, Dan Bryant and everybody in this panel, because I know everybody here is committed to what we are committed to—and that is justice in the case of the Brothers to the Rescue.
>
> One of my primary roles as General Counsel of the Cuban American National Foundation is to oversee legal activities related to the goal of bringing Fidel

Castro to justice for his crimes against humanity. In connection with that work, I have studied the facts and the legal underpinnings of this murder, and it is my legal opinion that there exists sufficient evidence and legal basis for the criminal indictment of Fidel Castro. What we don't have is the will to do it. I believe it is in the hands of President Clinton and his administration to bring about this indictment.

There have been some interesting developments since the murder of these pilots. One of them was the decision by Judge King in the Southern District of Florida, a Federal judge that looked at all the evidence presented, and he came to the conclusion that the Cuban government was responsible for these murders. He is a very learned judge, and he took a great deal of time to write his opinion. I want to quote from his opinion, because I think it is important for everybody to know what this judge had to say:

"The government of Cuba, on February 24, 1996, in an outrageous contempt for international law and basic human rights, murdered four human beings in international airspace over the Florida Straits. The victims were Brothers to the Rescue pilots, flying two civilian, unarmed planes on a routine humanitarian mission"— this was a finding by a Federal judge—"searching for rafters in the waters between Cuba and the Florida keys.

As the civilian planes flew over international waters, a Russian-built MiG 29 of the Cuban Air Force, without warning, reason or provocation, blasted the defenseless planes out of the sky with sophisticated air-to-air missiles in two separate attacks. The pilots and their aircraft disintegrated in the midair explosions following the impact of the missile. The destruction was so complete that the four bodies were never recovered."

A Federal Court of the United States of America so found, and we have no indictment yet of Mr. Castro. That murder occurred, according to our statutes, the Federal murder statute, 18 United States Code 111, cannot be denied, and it defines murder as the "unlawful killing of a human being with malice aforethought." That is what happened here.

Since that decision, more interesting things have happened, and you touched on it, Mr. McCollum. The United States Attorney for the Southern District of Florida and the FBI announced a superseding indictment in connection with the case of those Castro spies, and they added a charge of conspiracy to perpetrate murder in connection with the shootdown of the planes and charged one Gerardo Hernandez with conspiracy to commit murder within the special maritime and territorial jurisdiction of the United States, the same statute that I referred to earlier.

The indictment states that Hernandez and others, known and unknown to the grand jury, entered into a conspiracy whose object was to support and to help implement a plan for violent confrontation of BTTR aircraft with decisive and fatal results. Who was Gerardo Hernandez conspiring with? He was conspiring with his boss, Fidel Castro.

The indictment further states that in late January the Cuban Directorate of Intelligence reported approval by superior headquarters of *Operación Escorpión* in order to confront Brothers to the Rescue, cause a confrontation with them, and conveyed instructions from Miami agents which included informing on their flight data.

The indictment also states a Cuban agent, Juan Pablo Roque, was tasked and did in fact penetrate and inform on the Brothers to the Rescue. He was working for Castro as a spy, and he departed as part of the plot the day before the downing of the planes. He left Miami, left his wife behind, and went back to Cuba.

That was part of a plan, and Mr. Iglesias will develop that. But the indictment alludes to it.

After the shootdown, according to the indictment, the Cuban Directorate of Intelligence recognized Hernandez for his role and announced his promotion to Captain for his job in connection with the downing of the planes and the murder of these people. The Directorate of Intelligence noted that Fidel Castro, the commander in chief, had visited twice to analyze steps to follow up on the operation and had declared that they had dealt a hard blow to the Miami right.

So this indictment is a step in the right direction. I want to think that they are moving towards an indictment of Fidel Castro. They mention Fidel Castro in the indictment, but they indict Gerardo Hernandez. That is like indicting the monkey, not the organ grinder. What we need here is an indictment of Fidel Castro, not of his spies. The man who ordered this was Fidel Castro.

The only action that could provide any sense of justice to these people and to the people who died and to their families is the indictment of Fidel Castro. I certainly hope that our government is working towards that end.

It has been over three years though, Mr. McCollum. Can there be any doubt in the minds of any reasonable person, any reasonable juror, that Castro, who involves himself in the most minute and ridiculous details of

Cuban affairs, did not give the order to shoot the planes down? No, there cannot be.

The circumstantial evidence is formidable. You are going to hear the statement of Adel Regalado Ulloa, through his lawyer, because he still is cooperating with the FBI. He will provide specific details about the training that Castro's pilots had to shoot slow-moving targets, like an unarmed Cessna, and he will provide testimony through his lawyer to that effect.

They actually trained to shoot two little Cessnas. You will hear the testimony of Lázaro Betancourt Morin, who just showed up a few minutes ago, the most recent defector from Castro's security, a captain, confirming beyond any doubt that an order of this nature had to be planned and approved by Fidel Castro himself.

You will see the transcript of the radio communications between the Cuban MiG 29 and the ground control in Cuba asking for authorization. Castro had already ordered the shootdown, but just in case they asked for authorization and they got it, and they shot down these planes.

We have transcripts of the testimony from Robert White and Eugene Carroll, a former U.S. Navy Admiral, who stated that in the days before the downing of the plane they met with the Chief of Staff of the Cuban military, one General Rosales del Toro, who asked them, "What would you do"—meaning what would the United States do—"if we shot down the planes?" The question is: We are going to shoot them down. What is your response?

Well, they must have not been told anything that really frightened them, because they shot the planes down anyways.

Beyond the circumstantial evidence is, of course, the direct evidence from Fidel Castro himself. As you have pointed out and Representative Diaz-Balart pointed out, Castro admitted in the Time Magazine interview with Reginald K. Brack, Jr., the chairman of Time, Inc., that he ordered the downing of the planes. He met with his brother, Raúl Castro, as big a murderer as he is, and ordered the downing of the planes. He admitted responsibility. So we have all this great circumstantial evidence, and don't need much more. The man admitted that he did it, and we don't have an indictment against him.

I am confident the information we are going to present in this hearing is only but the tip of the iceberg of the information that the applicable and pertinent law enforcement agencies that work on this case have, but that evidence is sufficient to bring in an indictment.

Besides the murder statute, the statute I believe should be considered is what is known as the anti-terrorism statute, which is embodied in 18 United States Code section 2332, which provides a Federal criminal offense for the murder or conspiracy to murder a U.S. national while that national is outside the United States. This was enacted years back in order to go beyond the territorial waters of the United States and in a foreign country when involved in an act of terrorism. That statute is very clear and very well defined, homicide and conspiracy. You can indict Castro for either one or both.

There are some procedural considerations under this particular statute, this anti-terrorism statute, and that is that it requires a statutory certification by the Attorney General under section (d) that the offense was intended to coerce, intimidate or retaliate against a government or a civilian population. Fortunately for Attorney

General Janet Reno, that certification has been satisfied.

In the Cuban Liberty and Democratic Solidarity Act of 1996, the Libertad Act, the United States Congress made specific findings that the attack was timed in order to intimidate against the meeting of Concilio Cubano. You might remember on the day of the downings of the planes, the murder of the pilots, a group of peaceful human rights activists called Concilio Cubano were meeting, and the purpose of this downing was to intimidate them, is Castro's way of telling them and his own people that if you speak up against my government, I will kill you. Look, I am going to kill American citizens, and nothing is going to happen to me, and he did it.

Another issue that I think you might need to touch upon is the 'head of state' immunity, which is an issue that has to be resolved because, whether we like it or not, Castro is the dictator or president of Cuba.

We don't have a problem here. The practice of asserting extra territorial jurisdiction over persons domiciled in a foreign soil subject to a United States warrant is accepted, and we have the latest example of the case involving the dictator Manuel Noriega, where he was brought to the United—indicted and brought to the United States for his crimes. That is because his crimes, like Castro's crimes, were ultra vires. They were illegal acts. They are not part of the acts of a regular sitting president or prime minister of a government, lawful acts or acts in order to protect a sovereign nation.

The communications between the MiG-29 and Havana clearly showed that they knew that these were defenseless people, little-bitty Cessnas flying without any weapons. There was no threat to the Cuban people or to the government. This was an act by Fidel Castro that was an illegal act, and he enjoys no immunity when he acts illegally and criminally.

That is why Manuel Noriega is in jail today, because his crimes related to drug dealing. They have nothing to do with the affairs of state. They had to do with enriching himself.

Now, in the Noriega case, the 11th Circuit Court of Appeals said, all right, we don't have a sovereign immunity problem like the Foreign Sovereign Immunity Act, the head of state immunity does not find a formal basis in U.S. Law. What the Court of Appeals said is you look to the executive branch, and they realized that, in that case, they had sent troops, picked up the man and brought him here for a crime.

We need the executive branch of this country, we need President Clinton, the State Department, to say that Fidel Castro does not enjoy immunity as head of state for these crimes. These are ultra vires, illegal crimes. He needs to do that.

When he does that, he gives the green light to the U.S. Attorney for the Southern District of Florida to add one name to the indictment presently pending, that of Fidel Castro. That is what needs to happen here.

I will just touch upon one case, which is Jimenez v. Aristeguieta, where the 5th Circuit Court of Appeals rejected claims of a former Venezuelan dictator whose extradition was being challenged. He said all of his acts while he was a dictator were acts of state which precluded prosecution. The court rejected that and said, no, those acts were for his own benefit. Like Castro's act was for his own benefit, to stay in power. He has stayed in power for forty years. He has done it by killing people. That is how he stayed in power. That is not an act of the state that needs protection or immunity.

I am going to conclude by telling you that on one of the flights carried out by the Brothers to the Rescue, they entitled it, interestingly, "Martin Luther King, Jr." That was the name of the operation they gave it, and it was appropriate, because in that trip, on January 13th, 1996, they blanketed the City of Havana with leaflets urging nonviolent resistance, which is what Martin Luther King stood for and stands for today.

Now, after the Rosa Parks arrest, Martin Luther King was quoted as saying, **"If we are wrong, justice is a lie, and we are determined here in Montgomery to work and fight until justice runs down like water."**

Let there be no doubt that we do not believe that in America justice is a lie, and that we will likewise work and fight until justice runs down like water and Fidel Castro is brought to account for all his crimes against humanity.

At the mock trial, we presented evidence that top-level Cuban military officials asked U.S. officials prior to the shootdown how the United States would react if Cuba shot down the Brothers' planes. We showed how the Cuban MiGs sought and were granted authorization to shoot down the Brothers' planes and how Cuban ground control congratulated the MiG pilots after the unarmed planes had been destroyed.

We also presented evidence that Juan Pablo Roque, a spy who infiltrated the Brothers to the Rescue and fled back to Cuba just hours before the shootdown, was promoted within the Cuban military upon his return. We showed how Fidel Castro admitted to giving the order to the head of the Cuban Air Force to shoot down the planes.

We had the support of various congressmen and women,

including Congresswoman Ileana Ros-Lehtinen, a knowledge-able enemy of Castro. Her statement was particularly insightful:

On July 24, 1996, eight patriots boarded Brothers to the Rescue planes as they had done so many times before. They were embarking on a search of the Atlantic Ocean and the Caribbean, combing the waters for Cuban refugees who risk their lives in makeshift rafts in search of freedom and liberty.

On that fateful afternoon, the ruthless nature of the Castro regime was clearly revealed. Like vultures await-ing their prey, Cuban MiGs circled and hovered until they locked on to the frail Cessna planes. They shot down two of the planes carrying Carlos Acosta, Armando Alejandre, Mario de la Peña, and Pablo Morales. Not satisfied with the death of these courageous men, they engaged in a hostile pursuit of the third aircraft carrying two of the witnesses who are with us today (Basulto and Iriondo). And they are indeed fortunate to be alive.

We know who is ultimately responsible for this bla-tant act of aggression. Yet the Department of Justice has yet to conclude its investigation and issue indictments against the Castro regime for this criminal act. . . .

Information is available that confirms that U.S. radars picked up the Cuban MiGs early enough to scramble aircraft prior to the first Brothers to the Rescue plane being shot down. The MiGs were sighted by the U.S. at 3:01 p.m. The first plane was shot at 3:22 p.m. That means a twenty-one minute lapse time.

For that battle station alert, the response time for U.S. aircraft from Key West would be eleven minutes. On alert, it is estimated at five minutes. This indicates that, at the very least, there was ample time to prevent the deaths of the third and fourth victims and to provide protection to the last defenseless aircraft piloted by Jose Basulto who joins us today.

There would be no response, however, from the U.S. There would be no outrage or unconditional condemnation. In fact, Administration officials would not even classify the act as a terrorist act.

Serious questions remain about the U.S. role and actions prior, during, and after the attack. I hope that this hearing will shed some light on these unresolved matters as we continue to seek justice for all who have been victimized by the Castro regime, especially on that fateful day in 1996.

Compelling testimony was given by Jeffrey Houlihan, Senior Detection System Specialist at the Domestic Air Interdiction Coordination Center of the U.S. Customs Service. He monitored the ill-fated Brothers to the Rescue flight as they headed toward Cuba on the day of the shootdown. A little after 2:00 p.m., he picked up radar contact on the Brothers to the Rescue aircraft as they headed southbound toward Cuba. At around 3:00 p.m., he received radar information on two high-speed primary targets. What he saw were Castro's interceptor aircraft.

Houlihan assumed by their speed and maneuvering and that the two targets were Cuban MiGs. In the two years that he had been monitoring that area, Houlihan had never once before seen MiGs. The Brothers to the Rescue had been outspoken about their plans to fly toward Cuba that day, so Houlihan assumed the Cuban government was dispatching a combat air patrol to shoo the aircraft away from Cuba. He predicted that the MiGs would stay within Cuban territory and simply deter the Brothers to the Rescue aircraft from breaking into their airspace.

At about 3:16 p.m., one of the Cuban MiGs flew outside the

Cuban air defense identification zone and went directly over the top of the three Brothers to the Rescue aircraft. This worried Houlihan, as he had not expected them to leave the zone. He stated that seeing armed high-speed jets headed directly toward the Florida Keys *"going right over the U.S. registered aircraft concerned me."*

Believing that this was an air defense emergency, Houlihan immediately called the Southeast Air Defense Sector in Tyndall Air Force Base in Florida. Houlihan asked them if they knew what was going on with the Brothers to the Rescue planes. A representative at Tyndall replied that they were seeing the same thing he was and were handling it.

Houlihan testified that one of the Brothers to the Rescue planes, the one flown by José Basulto, penetrated the Cuban air defense identification zone—the twelve-mile limit around Cuba and their legal airspace—and proceeded eastbound for about a mile. The furthest Basulto ever got inside Cuban airspace was three nautical miles. The second Brothers to the Rescue plane stayed one nautical mile north of the Cuban air defense zone and the third one was about six miles out. They all began to head eastbound.

A little after 3:20 p.m., Houlihan saw one of the Cuban MiGs approach one of the Brothers to the Rescue planes. As the MiG passed by, the Brothers to the Rescue aircraft disappeared. Startled, Houlihan immediately yelled to the South Florida controller that it looked like a shootdown. A worker there named Tracy responded, *"Yes, I think it was."*

Houlihan directed Tracy to call the FAA immediately and find out what was going on. Houlihan then saw Basulto's aircraft start to maneuver inside the Cuban air defense zone and then go northward towards the United States.

The third Brothers to the Rescue aircraft went westbound and then came back eastbound for a few miles. It looked to

Houlihan like the pilot had seen the smoke from the first aircraft being shot down and turned northbound, running for the United States. Alarmed, Houlihan picked up the phone to call the Air Force again as the third Brothers to the Rescue aircraft continued northbound. The aircraft was about sixteen nautical miles north of the Cuban air defense zone when it disappeared. Right after it vanished, Houlihan picked up the Cuban MiG again in the same location, now heading southbound toward Cuba.

Houlihan asked, *"Did you see what I saw? It looks like those two airplanes were shot down."*

The Air Force representative refused to speak to Houlihan because he wasn't on a secure line.

We cross-referenced the U.S. Air Force radar print screens and location data with the transcripts of the Cuban MiGs and their controllers. Both documents concur that the third Brothers to the Rescue aircraft was well to the north of the twenty-fourth parallel and that the Cuban MiGs were within three minutes of reaching the United States. There is clear evidence that at least one of the MiGs crossed the twenty-fourth parallel into U.S. air territory.

I brought in José Basulto—President of the Brothers to the Rescue and leader of the ill-fated mission—to testify. A brave man and a strong ally, Basulto is one of the leading figures of the anti-Castro movement. His testimony was crucial because his plane was able to escape and he had more facts on hand than anyone else.

José understood that my intention was to ultimately convince our government that Fidel Castro should be indicted. Unfortunately, he was also determined to present evidence of his belief that the Clinton Administration had sanctioned the shoot-down of the planes. It was a mighty struggle to keep him focused on my goal.

José gave a dramatic account of the shootdown from his perspective. Although he was the main target of the attack, he managed to escape by flying into heavy cloud cover. He felt guilty for surviving while his friends perished. He complained bitterly about the Clinton Administration's refusal to bring criminal charges against Castro. He advanced the notion that the members of the Administration were accomplices in the murders and that its witnesses shielded themselves under the privilege of national security to hide their guilt. He asked for the Sub-Committee to subpoena those involved.

I could not control José then. I don't think anybody can to this day. He was just as angry at the Clinton Administration as he was at the Castro brothers—and I can understand why. His testimony was truthful and consistent with the evidence and documentation of the event. I believe Clinton had a personal relationship with Fidel Castro because of the Brothers to the Rescue shootdown, and I firmly agree with José Basulto that Clinton turned a blind eye during the incident.

José pointed out that his airplane only escaped after an uninterrupted fifty-three minute chase. During this period of time, the Cuban MiGs shot down two Brothers to the Rescue planes in international airspace. Members of the U.S. military were on alert that day to monitor the Brothers to the Rescue flights. They watched these events unfold on radar and heard the radio broadcasts and pleas for help. Nevertheless, they did not act. Even as the planes were shot down, they remained in absolute silence. Did they not have a responsibility to protect U.S. lives, property, and national security?

José had to courage to ask, "*Why did this happen?*" It was a good question.

The facts developed at this hearing were quite alarming. It appeared that the Clinton Administration had prior knowledge that Castro was planning the attack on the Brothers to the

Rescue planes, yet it never informed the pilots or the organization. In January 1996, U.S. intelligence agencies spotted Cuban MiGs conducting practice maneuvers in which they test-fired air-to-air missiles against slow-moving aircraft similar to Brothers to the Recue planes. One of our witnesses, Abel Regalado Ulloa, attested to this training. Basulto rightfully complained that Brothers to the Rescue was not advised of the practice maneuvers.

Silvia Iriondo, another leading figure of the anti-Castro movement, had been in the plane with Basulto and also testified in the case. She is the President of MAR, a women's organization that champions the cause of freedom in Cuba. Silvia Iriondo had proof that the murder of these four men was premeditated—she testified about the activities of Juan Pablo Roque, one of Castro's spies.

According to Ms. Iriondo, Roque befriended members of Brothers to the Rescue and was taken in as a friend and collaborator. It turned out that he was acting on the orders of Fidel Castro to infiltrate the humanitarian group and help orchestrate the shootdown. Only one day before the attack, Juan Pablo Roque returned to Cuba, leaving his wife in Florida behind. News of his escape made the front page of the Miami Herald.

The dictator's plan was thwarted, according to Ms. Iriondo, because their plane survived and they were in a position to disprove Roque's lies. Castro's plan was to shoot down all three planes—leaving no witnesses—so that Juan Pablo Roque could claim that the Brothers to the Rescue had carried out terrorist actions against the Castro government. This would have given Castro immunity from prosecution. Ms. Iriondo's testimony was consistent with the evidence presented. Roque's involvement showed that the shootdown was in fact a well-orchestrated plan.

Fidel Castro himself acknowledged that he had given the order to kill in his interview with *Time Magazine*.

The testimony of Lázaro Betancourt Morin, then a recent Cuban defector, was especially informative. Morin was a former captain of Castro's Special Mission Command and a specialist in anti-kidnapping and anti-terrorist techniques who served for twenty years in the Special Forces of the Minister of the Interior of the Republic of Cuba. Morin testified at the hearing that the order to shoot down the Brothers to the Rescue planes could only have come from Fidel Castro. He said that this account was consistent with his work for the Castro government.

Congressman Bill McCollum, Chairman of the Congressional Committee that hosted the mock trial, declared that the Committee unanimously found Fidel Castro guilty of the murders related to the Brothers to the Rescue.

The hearing proved beyond doubt that Fidel Castro ordered the downing of the planes and that he should be indicted under U.S. law for murder. However, this would only occur if the President of the United States supports the indictment. It is still possible to do so. As a murder charge, it has no statute of limitations. There is clear jurisdiction because Cuban spies were actively working to carry out the murder in the U.S., and Castro himself admitted to ordering the shootdown. Moreover, the circumstantial evidence proves beyond reasonable doubt that only Castro could have given the order.

Regrettably, the hearing also raised the possibility that our government was well aware of the possibility of a shootdown. Why didn't the United States send its own planes to intercept Castro's MiGs as they approached U.S. airspace? There is no conceivable explanation. We don't let enemy fighter planes within ten miles of our shore and not respond.

On August 3, 1999, about two weeks after I presented a case for his criminal indictment for murder in the U.S. Congress, I received calls from friends at about 3:00 a.m. saying Fidel was talking about me. He had been ranting on since 9:00 p.m. the day before. I quote from his tirade against the Foundation:

The leadership of the Foundation has been composed almost in its totality by elements of (people) related in some form to the Batista dictatorship or affected in a significant way by the revolutionary laws. This time, as an example, after the death of Mas Canosa, we can mention the following examples: Francisco Jose Hernandez, who until a few days ago was the President of the Foundation when he was substituted by Jorge Mas Santos. He is the son of Lieutenant Colonel Francisco Hernandez Leyva, condemned to death by a court in Santa Clara in 1959 for war crimes during the Batista dictatorship; Roberto Martin Perez, member of the Executive Committee (of the Foundation) and head of the paramilitary group of the Foundation. He is the son of the well known Batista esbirro (thug) Lutgardo Martin Perez, who was able to escape to the United States; Ninoska Perez Castellon, a Director and the voice of the Foundation. She is the daughter of Lieutenant Colonel Francisco Perez Gonzalez, second chief of the bloody radio motor section of the Batista police in Havana, who also left the country towards the United States. **Jorge Fowler, attorney of the Foundation, son of the plantation owner of the same name, owner of 1,900 caballerías (62,000 acres) of land in Cuba and of the sugar mill Narcisa.**

I was glad to hear that Castro had mentioned me. It meant that our efforts for his criminal indictment were of concern to him. It was his way of trying to intimidate me.

THE DEFECTION OF LÁZARO BETANCOURT MORIN

ON APRIL 16, 1999, AT THE SECOND SUMMIT OF THE PRESIDENTS the Caribbean countries in the Dominican Republic, one of Castro's bodyguards, Lázaro Betancourt Morin, defected. Morin abandoned his security measures and went to the U.S. Embassy, seeking political asylum. Once he heard of the defection, Castro panicked and left in the middle of a visit with the President of the Dominican Republic. This was Castro's final public international trip. I met Morin. He is a short, powerful man obviously trained to kill.

Morin gave valuable testimony regarding Castro's chain of command that proved beyond doubt that Castro ordered the Brothers to the Rescue murders. However, he also provided interesting information about Castro's fear of the Foundation and indictment. While our efforts to hunt down Castro so far have not succeeded, they have greatly unsettled him.

At the mock trial of Castro before the House of Representatives, Morin testified about work I had done with the Foundation and the *Audiencia Nacional*. Castro was very concerned about his personal security when he traveled abroad because he knew we were looking for him:

I was selected on seven occasions to become a member of the security and protection division to the president, the

Cuban president Fidel Castro, on his visits to the foreign countries beginning in 1989 up to date where the assault group which I belong to had the irrevocable order of using any kind of force and means to any action anywhere in the world against the life of Fidel Castro, specifically any legal proceeding, an attempt to his life, or of kidnapping him, or any court order. Similarly, what is going on to the former Chilean President and Senator Augusto Pinochet, making all kind of efforts in the measures to prevent any of these occasions that as per them it would come from the Cuban American National Foundation directed by the CIA. Also as a result of legal proceedings anywhere in the world.

It was Morin's job to do everything possible—including murder—to keep Castro from being arrested or detained.

At a news conference in Miami, Morin told reporters that no one else on the island has the kind of security that Castro enjoys, and that there are no orders to safeguard his successors. According to Morin, Castro greatly fears being indicted and considers the Foundation to be his biggest enemy.

I think Castro is right to be afraid. Sooner or later, he will have to account for his crimes.

LOS CINCO (THE FIVE)

LOS CINCO—ALSO KNOWN AS THE CUBAN FIVE OR THE MIAMI Five—were a group of Cuban intelligence officers employed by Castro to help orchestrate the downing of the Brothers to the Rescue planes. In 2001, they were convicted in Miami of conspiracy to commit espionage and murder.

Juan Pablo Roque, the spy who escaped, infiltrated the Brothers to the Rescue and flew several missions. On February 26, 1996, Roque appeared on Cuban television and falsely claimed that the Brothers to the Rescue planned to introduce anti-personnel weapons to Cuba. The sheer brazenness of his actions was amazing. While living in Miami, Roque repeatedly made contact with the FBI. He married a woman in Miami who he later abandoned. His wife thought it was a real marriage, but it turned out that he had a family in Cuba.

Roque now lives in Havana and remains free to this day.

The Five are Gerardo Hernández, Antonio Guerrero, Ramon Lavanino, Fernando González, and René González. They went to the United States at Castro's behest to infiltrate the U.S. Southern Command, the Cuban American National Foundation, the Brothers to the Rescue, and Alpha 66, a more militant anti-Castro group. At the trial, Guy Lewis presented evidence that the Five infiltrated the Brothers to the Rescue and obtained employment at the Key West Naval Air Station. Their objectives were to report the activities of the base to Cuba and to monitor Basulto's flights.

Castro admitted that the Five were intelligence agents, but he claimed their job was to spy on Miami's Cuban exile community—not the U.S. government. Castro often sends agents to infiltrate anti-Castro organizations; we have found this out for ourselves. Castro has been tempted by the possibility of inserting agents into the membership and directorship of the Foundation. Over the years, I have even suspected employees at my law firm of being moles.

Castro is careful not to give the U.S. enough reason to invade the island. He toes the line but never steps over it.

The Miami U.S. Attorney at the time, Guy Lewis, called to let me know the date of the sentencing. I was able to attend and look them in the eye right before they were sentenced. In this case, justice was done. For this, I credit Lewis, an American with a Cuban wife who well understands Castro's Cuba. We have teamed up together in cases.

It was some consolation for me to know that Castro's spies had been caught and imprisoned. I continue to hope that one of them will turn on Castro and finger him for directing the Brothers to the Rescue murders.

Once the five spies were convicted and imprisoned in the U.S., Castro waged a relentless campaign to return them to Cuba. However, Castro must have known that the U.S. government would never acquiesce to his demands so easily. Nervous that the Cuban Five might testify against him, Castro's true intention was to let them know that he is still watching them—even in prison—and that their families in Cuba are at risk. Vintage Castro terror tactics.

While we felt some vindication, the indictment of the five spies fell woefully short of what should have been done. Fidel

Castro himself should have been indicted. Through the work of his spies and his military, Castro murdered three Americans with impunity. Castro had agents operating in the United States and plotting the murder of U.S. citizens, yet somehow the master-mind faced no consequences. It was yet another example of our government's unwillingness to stop Castro's terrorism.

On August 21, 2003, then-U.S. Attorney Marcos Daniel Jiménez, and Guy Lewis's successor, opened a grand jury indict-ment. The charges were brought against Rubén Martínez Puente, a general in Castro's Air Force, and jet fighter pilots Lorenzo Alberto Peréz-Peréz and Francisco Peréz-Peréz. These three, working in concert with Cuba's Director of Intelligence, were the men responsible for shooting down the Brothers to the Rescue planes. Jiménez indicted them for conspiracy to kill U.S. nationals. The conspiracy, known in the indictment as "Operation Escorpión," included Cuban spy sources from with-in the Southern District of Florida:

> The goal of which was to terrorize, intimidate, and retal-
> iate against the Cuban exile community as well as to
> intimidate the Cuban populace, through a violent con-
> frontation with aircraft operated by the Brothers to the
> Rescue, with decisive and fatal results.

The two pilots, Lorenzo Alberto Peréz-Peréz and Francisco Peréz-Peréz, followed the instructions of General Rubén Martínez Puente, who was given the go-ahead by Fidel Castro.

In the recordings, the pilots alluded to their *cojones*, or in English, "balls." The former U.S. Ambassador to the United Nations, Madeleine Albright, denounced the Cuban govern-ment before the United Nations and said, "*This is not cojones. It is cowardice.*"

In October 2011, after completing thirteen years of his sentence, René González was released but kept in the United States on probation. The Castro government made a tremendous effort to bring González back to Cuba. Ricardo Alarcón, head of Cuba's National Assembly, sardonically said that if anything happens to René González, the United States government is probably responsible. The hypocrites in Cuba are quick to predict that our government will resort to murder. René González is now back in Cuba; the Obama Administration released the murderer before he completed his sentence.

Why has our government allowed Castro to cause so much damage to our people and to endanger our national security? This is a question to which I can provide no answer.

THE ELIÁN GONZÁLEZ AFFAIR

WHEN I GO BACK TO CUBA, I'M GOING TO SEEK OUT ELIÁN González's father, Juan Miguel. Once I see him, I'm giving him a hard kick in his cowardly ass for giving up his little boy to the monster in Havana.

In November 1999, Elizabeth Brotons, left Cuba in a tiny aluminum boat with the hopes of bringing her little boy, Elián, to the United States to live in freedom. She tragically drowned in a storm en route, but little Elián miraculously survived. When he made it to the United States, he was joyfully reconnected with his extended family in Florida. However, due to an absurd legal battle waged by Attorney General Janet Reno at the direction of Bill Clinton, federal agents seized little Elián—grabbing him from his relatives at gunpoint—and returned him to the dictator in June of 2000.

As the lawyer for the Foundation, I was permitted to join the family's legal team, led by Armando Gutiérrez, the self-appointed family spokesperson. Our mission was to fight the Clinton Administration's efforts to send the boy back to Cuba so he could legally stay in the U.S. as his mother wished. The lead counsel was Kendal Coffey, a prominent Miami attorney and a former U.S. Attorney. His partner was Manny Diaz, a friend who later became Mayor of Miami. The team was rounded out with several other influential lawyers including Spencer Eig, Linda Osberg Braun, Alberto Mora, Geoffrey J. Greeves, Ronald W. Kleinman, Jose Garcia-Pedrosa, Barbara Lagoa, and my friend and former classmate, Richard Sharpstein.

Although I was glad to be part of the effort, it was an extremely frustrating experience. The Clinton Administration was dead set on returning Elián to Cuba. They spared no effort. Perhaps because I was not initially appointed to the team, I did not have an influential voice in the strategy. At the last moment, when it became clear the courts would send Elián back, I was allowed to act.

I filed an action in Washington, D.C., seeking an order to prevent the U.S. Government from returning Elián to Cuba. I argued that our government was signatory to international treaties that prohibited it from sending Elián back to a country known for violating human rights. The court agreed with my argument, but correctly held that it should have been filed in the main case in Miami.

For me, and for hundreds of thousands of other Cuban exiles, the Elián González affair was one of the most negative experiences in recent memory. I was involved in this case from beginning to bitter end. When other lawyers in New Orleans noticed my long absences and many TV appearances, rumors even began to spread that I had abandoned my practice. I certainly devoted a great deal of time to the case, but my friends and clients stuck by me. They knew the depth of my commitment and respected me for what I was doing.

The Elián González affair was particularly hard for Cubans who lived in Miami where the newspapers and radio actually tell the truth about Cuba. My friends and relatives there had the mistaken impression that most Americans actually understood the issues. After all, it's hard to understand why anyone would want to take a little boy away from the freedom his mother died for and give him up to a dictator. (I knew better though; in New Orleans, all that is printed about Cuba are superficial editorials from the *Times-Picayune* calling for the end to the embargo.)

Let's review the case. Little Elián, his mother, and twelve others escaped Cuba on a small boat with a problematic engine. During this dangerous crossing—one that has been daringly made by thousands of freedom-loving Cubans—González's mother drowned in a storm. Ten others also died in the escape attempt.

Later, Elián told Marisleysis, his cousin, that the boat's motor had broken and the passengers tried in vain to bail out the water. Unfortunately they were beset by a storm, and Elizabeth's boyfriend placed Elián in an inner tube for safety. Elián never saw his mother again. Nivaldo Fernández Ferran, one of the three survivors, said that Elizabeth protected Elián to the end.

I spent a good deal of time with Donato Dalrymple, one of the two fishermen who rescued Elián and a man of great faith. Donato sported a crew cut and was always a source of great amusement to me. One time, we were in the middle of a tense, all-night negotiation. Senator Torricelli, Jorge Mas Santos, and I were on one line, and U.S. Attorney General Janet Reno was on the other. When I turned to Donato, he had fallen asleep!

Donato didn't care about all the big names involved in the case; he was more impressed by that fateful day on the water. He and his cousin were fishing when they spotted the inner tube floating in the water, and at first they didn't realize it contained a little boy. Finally, they saw a hand poke out. Large sharks were circling the inner tube, and Donato feared for the boy's life. As he got closer, he realized that porpoises were deliberately bumping the sharks away to keep the little boy safe.

Donato described it as a mystical, miraculous scene. He made it clear that he believed it was a miracle and that God stepped in to protect the boy. As a strong Catholic, I have no doubt that God intervened for little Elián.

Under our bizarre, ridiculous, and heartless immigration policy—the "wet feet, dry feet" rule—any Cuban found at sea attempting to reach our coast will be arrested and immediately returned to Cuba into the hands of the cruel dictator. This happens regularly to this day. Refugees can plead for political asylum only if they can make it to shore. Theoretically, if you are a good swimmer and can beat the Coast Guard to land, you can stay. If not, you will face Castro's "justice." Little Elián made it to the United States and had the right to stay in freedom, but it was not to be. Bill Clinton was determined to send the boy back to Cuba. The Clinton Administration claimed only his father could decide whether he stayed or not, but the father was controlled by Castro. The father demanded that Elián be returned to him in Cuba.

Once the Immigration and Naturalization Service released Elián to his paternal great-uncle Lázaro, Castro and Clinton started plotting how to bring him back. Marisleysis and Lázaro told me that Elián's father, Juan Miguel González Quintana, called Lázaro on November 22 to say that Elián and his mother had left Cuba and to watch out for their arrival. According to the family, Juan Miguel told them to wait for him and that he would come to the United States to be with his son "even if he had to get there on a bathtub." At that moment, he too wanted freedom in the U.S.

Once the case became a cause célèbre, Fidel Castro took control of the cowardly Juan Miguel. Elián's father pulled a 180° and suddenly started publicly demanding the return of his son to Cuba. Lázaro and the rest of the family said that they wanted the little boy to live in freedom, and Marisleysis took care of little Elián. The struggle began and became headline news every day for months.

Jorge Mas Santos and I visited the family regularly to offer the Foundation's support. Their little house in Miami was constantly surrounded by hundreds of reporters. One day, as I was talking to Elián in Lázaro's backyard, Marisleysis came out with a phone in her hand and told Elián that his father wanted to speak to him. Elián burst out crying and ran away, saying he didn't want to. The little boy was not acting; those were his true feelings. It was the emotional reaction of a boy whose father had paid no attention to him, whose mother had died trying to bring him to freedom.

Although I committed myself to doing everything I could to allow Elián to live in freedom, deep down in my heart I knew that the legal strategy would end in failure. It was like watching a slow-moving train about to crash. To make the best of it, I devoted time to making TV appearances. That way I could denounce Castro's crimes against humanity in front of a national audience.

The Elián González story was the main news story in the early months of 2000. I appeared regularly on CNN's *Burden of Proof* with Greta Van Sustern. I also appeared on Geraldo Rivera's show and on *Both Sides with Jesse Jackson*, among many others. I debated dozens of liberal congressmen and members of the media. Most of them had no notion of where Cuba was located, much less what it meant to send a little boy back to Castro. My only hope was to try to educate people about the horrors of the regime.

Every once in a while I'd take a shot at Bill Clinton for his failures during and after the Brothers to the Rescue shootdown. I also noted that Clinton's lawyer, Greg Craig—who represented him in the Monica Lewinsky impeachment trial—became Elián's father's lawyer during this episode. Since Castro controlled Elián's father, this meant that Craig was effectively Castro's lawyer. Craig even traveled to meet Castro in Cuba to design his legal strategy.

It was baffling to me, and to thousands of other Cuban Americans, that our country would actually fight to return this boy to Castro. The Cuban exiles were shocked when they learned that a majority of Americans thought the boy should go back to his father in Cuba.

After I appeared on Greta's show, we started referring to CNN as the Communist News Network or Castro News Network. Castro had offered them a deal: he would allow their reporters into Cuba so long as they reported favorably on the government. The network readily agreed to this bargain. The retired president of CNN actually admitted that this was the only way they could get into a country ruled by dictators. I don't recall being taught that when I studied journalism and ethics in college.

Greta spread the show's commentary between me and five leftist pundits. Often I would try to speak only to learn that my voice had been muted. The rest of the guests chatted among themselves about the ridiculous Cuban Americans and how the boy obviously should be returned to his father in Castro's Cuba. When I wasn't muted, it was five against one.

Fortunately, as a trial lawyer, I knew how to quickly spit out what I wanted to say and never answer any loaded questions. I was also armed with a powerful weapon that they didn't have: I actually knew what I was talking about. They had to look in an atlas to find out where Cuba was. Greta must have seen the light; she is now working for Fox News. Funny what a limo can do to a liberal mind.

Appearing on Geraldo Rivera's show was interesting. On my first appearance, he took it easy on me. The second time, he had Donato Dalrymple's cousin on the show. Donato's cousin was there when they found Elián, but he took the position that the boy should be returned to Cuba. I think his opinion had less to do with principles and more to do with the fact that the charismatic Donato got all the headlines.

I was on *Both Sides with Jesse Jackson* twice. I respect the Reverend. Once I heard both him and Jorge Mas Canosa give testimony regarding Cuba in Congress. Jesse Jackson spoke forcefully against the U.S. embargo, but Jorge Mas Canosa replied with an emotional, impassioned speech that left everyone breathless. It was so moving that Jesse, in my presence, walked over to Jorge, hugged him, and admitted to being wrong about what he had said.

One thing that troubled me greatly was that Elián's father didn't have the guts to come to Miami to see his son. If it had been my child, I would have been there in hours. Although I had no doubt that Castro was controlling him, I wanted to see if Juan Miguel really loved his boy. On television, I challenged him to come to Miami. I promised that the family would welcome his visit and that the boy could and should see his father. Obviously, he never came.

Under the dictator's direction, Elián's father eventually flew to Washington, D.C., and stayed with Castro's people at the Swiss Embassy. I flew to Washington with Lázaro's brother, the father's best friend, and Donato Dalrymple. For days, we stood outside the Swiss Embassy calling for Juan Miguel to come out to meet with Donato, the man who had saved his son's life. In addition to spreading the message through the media, I literally yelled for him to come down until my voice was hoarse.

The reporters picked up on the challenge and started asking why Juan Miguel wouldn't come out to meet Donato. Every once in a while, Juan Miguel, with two or three of Castro's thugs by his side, would come out and flick the bird at me or shout obscenities. He looked terrible, like a zombie, and we thought that he was probably under the influence of drugs.

Finally, I got a very unfriendly call from the father's lawyer, Greg Craig, who asked me if I was Donato Dalrymple's lawyer. After telling him I wasn't, I asked whether he thought Donato needed one. Mr. Craig didn't seem to think I was very funny. I argued that Donato just wanted to meet with Juan Miguel and tell him that his son was in good hands. I didn't tell him that Donato Dalrymple really wanted to convince him to defect and stay in the United States with his boy, which we had all arranged. Craig's rather rude response: *"The meeting will take place at my office tomorrow at 10:00 a.m.—or not at all."*

Down South, we lawyers treat each other with greater civility. I suggested we go to a nearby coffee house, but when he didn't bother to respond, I agreed to meet him at his office. The following day, Juan Miguel met with Donato Dalrymple. Craig did not give me the professional courtesy to attend the meeting. If it were on my terms, I would have welcomed Craig to my offices in New Orleans; I would have even offered him chicory coffee and beignets.

As expected, the meeting between Donato and Juan Miguel was short and perfunctory. We knew that it was only done to respond to the rising media pressure. After he was thrown out of Craig's office, Donato ran to the numerous reporters and cameras outside to grab the microphone and give his version of the story first. Just as we had planned. Donato told the reporters that he tried to tell Juan Miguel to stay in the United States with his boy in freedom, but was thrown out of Craig's office. I loved hanging around with Donato; we both were on the same page.

During these days in Washington, D.C., I also worked with Jorge Mas Santos and Senator Torricelli to negotiate a deal so that Juan Miguel could meet in peace with Elián, Lázaro, and his family. We wanted the meeting to last as long as possible in the hopes that the drugs would wear off and Juan Miguel would come to his senses. We proposed the Vatican Building, but not because it was neutral ground. The Vatican was an independent state, so Elián's father could seek political asylum there if he ever came to his senses. Janet Reno declined, however, and the meeting never took place.

Elián had two grandmothers. I call one the good grandmother (the mother of Elián's mother, Elizabeth Brotons, Raquel Rodríguez) and other the bad grandmother (Juan Miguel's mother, Mariela Quintana). After much negotiation, Castro permitted the two grandmothers to visit their grandson in the hopes of obtaining his return to Cuba. The meeting was arranged at the Miami Beach home of Sister Jeanne O'Laughlin, the President of Barry University. A firm advocate of the boy's return to Cuba, O'Laughlin also had no idea what she was talking about.

That was a psychedelic day. We arranged it so that Jorge Mas Santos brought Elián to Sister O'Laughlin's home in a car. Clara del Valle and I were in a home next door in the backyard. There were military planes, helicopters, and Navy boats patrolling the Miami Beach River, and thousands of reporters with cameras waited outside the home. Clara and I quietly conversed as we watched this amazing scene develop. We feared that either Castro or our government would use the opportunity to grab Elián and take him back to Cuba with the grandmothers. I am not sure exactly what we could have done to prevent it. As usual, we were witnesses to the chaos and irrationality that unfolded around us.

Then, surprisingly, Sister O'Laughlin came to the fence between the two homes and motioned for us to come over. She told us that Castro knew we were there and that the two grandmothers would not meet with Elián unless we left the premises. The owner of the house regretfully asked us to leave—he didn't want to start any trouble—so we left and faced the throng of reporters. We told them that Castro had kicked us out and taken control of the grandmothers' visit to Miami Beach. The meeting between the boy and his grandmothers soon took place.

Then, something happened that most people don't know about. Sister O'Laughlin suddenly changed her position and insisted that the boy should stay. It appears that she had an opportunity to visit with the mother's mother, Raquel Rodríguez. Raquel told Sister O'Laughlin that she wanted the little boy to stay in the United States but was petrified to tell anyone. Once she recognized the true situation, Sister O'Laughlin made a moral U-turn and argued that the boy should stay. I guess that as a religious person, she could recognize the presence of evil when she saw it.

Frustrated with the legal developments in the case, the Foundation made a desperate effort on Capitol Hill to keep Elián in the United States. We proposed Senate legislation that would override U.S. immigration laws and grant the boy and his family permanent resident status in the United States. We obtained the support of New Hampshire Republican Bob Smith, Florida Democrat Bob Graham, and Republican Connie Mack, who had previously submitted a bill to make Elián a U.S. citizen. Juan Miguel, always under the control of Fidel Castro, wrote an open letter to the Senate leaders saying that he did not want his son to become either a U.S. citizen or a permanent resident.

Senator Bob Graham (D–FL), a good friend of our cause, challenged then-Vice President Al Gore to act on his principles. At the time, Gore was planning his presidential run. He claimed to support Elián staying in the United States, knowing very well that the support of Cuban Americans in Florida was vital to winning the election. He also knew that supporting Bill Clinton's efforts to return the boy to Cuba would seriously damage his chances. So when Al Gore tried to distance himself from Bill Clinton's position, Senator Graham challenged him to do more than just talk:

First, let's clear up one misunderstanding. The Vice

President [Al Gore] has taken a consistent position since December that the case of Elián González should be treated not as an INS case but rather as a custody case in family court. The legislation that we have introduced has that as one of its principal objectives. If Elián were granted permanent legal residence in the United States, his case would be moved from the INS and would be placed in a family court where the question would be what is in Elián's best interest.

We lost by one vote, and thus the bill, introduced on March 29, 2000, died. By and large, the Democrats were against it—with the exceptions of our friends Bob Graham, Joe Lieberman, Harry Reid, and Robert Torricelli. Al Gore failed to support the bill and eventually lost his bid to become President of the United States.

On March 21, 2000, a federal court dismissed the relatives' petition for asylum for Elián. In Miami, Mayor Alex Penelas and many other civic leaders said that they would not cooperate with federal authorities if they decided to forcefully send the boy back to Cuba. We got one bit of good news when the Eleventh Circuit Court of Appeals in Atlanta held that, pending the appeal for asylum, Elián could stay in the United States. When Janet Reno threatened to forcefully return Elián to his father, the Cubans in Miami vowed to protect the little boy and surrounded the house.

On April 20, Reno instructed law enforcement officers to take the boy by force. In the early hours of April 22, eight SWAT-equipped agents, using pepper spray and mace, smashed into the house and found Donato holding on to little Elián in a closet. You may recall the famous picture of the agent pointing a gun at Donato and the little boy.

The day that Elián was seized at gunpoint happened to be

the same day I was scheduled to appear on Jesse Jackson's show. After hearing the news, I was livid. The other guest was Congressman Charles Rangel, a fan of Castro. When Rangel began his diatribe, I hollered at him with such anger that he actually shut up.

Since the father lacked the courage to travel to Florida and get his son himself, Elián was taken to Washington, D.C. Greg Craig then took Elián and Juan Miguel to a lavish dinner in the Georgetown mansion of Smith and Elizabeth Bagley, good friends of the Clintons.

On June 1, 2000, the Eleventh Circuit Court of Appeals decided that Elián was too young to file for asylum. It ruled that only his father could make that filing and that his relatives did not have standing to do so. The U.S. Supreme Court declined to review the decision. Later that day, little Elián was returned to Cuba. Since then, he has been a prisoner of Fidel Castro—just like every other citizen of Cuba, except that he is watched more carefully. It would be a great embarrassment if Elián González escaped Cuba and told the truth. I think that he will express his true feelings once he is free.

After the Elián González affair, I and many other influential Cuban Americans met to determine a strategy to better educate Americans on the situation in Cuba. My peers were truly alarmed by the public animosity that was shown toward Cuban Americans during the affair. In that meeting, Jorge Mas Santos and Leopoldo Fernández Pujols each pledged a million dollars to begin a public relations campaign; others offered more modest sums.

I thought then that even the most skilled media team, with an unlimited financial budget, wouldn't be able to change the mainstream view. Many liberal Americans dislike Cuban Americans because they are an immigrant group that is financially successful, mostly Republican, and politically powerful.

Liberals prefer their minority groups to have their palms up and seeking aid, so that once they provide that aid—with money made by others—they can feel good about themselves. This liberal element is unhappy with both successful Cuban Americans and successful people in general. That's the reason why President Obama was widely acclaimed when he said, "*If you've got a business, you didn't build that. Somebody else made that happen.*"

And that's the way I see it today.

THE SPLIT

AFTER JORGE MAS CANOSA PASSED AWAY, THERE WAS A VALIANT struggle to maintain the momentum and vibrancy of the Foundation, but to no avail. His death was a gut punch. Dr. Alberto Hernandez soon assumed the chairmanship of the Foundation in his place. He was no Jorge Mas Canosa, but he was passionate about the Foundation's work. The problem was that Jorge carried the cause on his shoulders, and upon his death the inevitable comparisons arose. The Foundation soon suffered from deep, internal strife—and ultimately there was a split.

Jorge Mas Canosa wanted his son, Jorge Mas Santos, to assume the leadership of the Foundation, even though he had not previously been a director. I, too, wanted a younger leader. Mas Santos had given an eloquent eulogy at his father's funeral. Bilingual, articulate, and highly intelligent, he was the perfect choice for the chairmanship, despite the fact that his father had held the position. (I viewed that as a negative, not a positive.) A skilled and capable businessman, Mas Santos is Chairman of the Board of MasTec, Inc. He and his two younger brothers—Jose, now CEO of MasTec, Inc., and Juan Carlos—make a strong team, and Mas Santos works hard for the success of his company.

In his day, Jorge Mas Canosa had coddled the Directors of the Foundation and ensured that generous contributors were given special treatment. In the 80s and early 90s, it was a high honor to be a Director of the Foundation, and there was always an area cordoned off for them at the various Miami functions. Clara del Valle and I found the hierarchy a bit ridiculous, but there was no doubt that it was useful—Jorge Mas Canosa could raise thousands of dollars for the cause in a single meeting. He would say something like, "We need money to support the effort in Washington, D.C. Without it, we will not get the required legislation passed. Therefore, I, Jorge Mas Canosa, will pledge $50,000." Right away, you would hear similar pledges from the Foundation's other directors. Everybody got a round of applause, and the checks were collected shortly thereafter.

I asked Jorge Mas Santos whether he would accept the chairmanship, and he told me that he would. Carlos Quintela, Remberto Perez, and I began an effort to replace Alberto Hernandez with Jorge Mas Santos, and the younger Jorge was soon unanimously elected to the position. Pepe continued as President, and he and Jorge soon forged a strong relationship.

Then the rift began. Some said that it was a split between the older generation and the more liberal members of the younger generation. It was certainly more complex than that. Arguments broke out, and eventually the conflict made the front pages of the Miami Herald.

I was livid. Although I fully understood that everyone had a right to their own opinion, the differences should have been aired within the confines of the Foundation. However, the dissenters were openly critical and even gave interviews to newspapers. The editors of the *Miami Herald* thoroughly enjoyed publishing stories about the strife; they still remembered when Mas Canosa had brought them to their knees.

In 2001, *The New York Times* published various articles savoring the defection. Take the following excerpt:

After more than 40 years of standing silently against Fidel Castro, the leading organization for Cuban exiles, the Cuban American National Foundation, was sundered today as nearly two dozen board members resigned. They contended that the group had forgotten its purpose and softened its line on Cuban issues.

Regrettably, the defecting board members decided to resign en masse and announced the news in a very public press conference. The defectors attacked Mas Santos without restraint and continued their assault on the radio and television. Their goal was to destroy the Foundation and create a new organization in its place. From my perspective, we lost a number of valuable directors including, Ninoska and Roberto Martin Perez.

Although unhappy with these developments, I tried to soften the blow. *The New York Times* quoted me as saying, "We have a young leader who is 38 years old, and he is not bound by old ideas and concepts, and he is going to be flexible. He has taken different and newer approaches, and some people are taking a very dim view of the changes."

The New York Times reported that a major source of conflict came in June when the Foundation's leaders met with Senator Joseph I. Lieberman after a fundraising dinner for the Florida Democratic Party in Miami. The defecting directors said that the Foundation should have declined the invitation to meet with Lieberman, who was Vice President Al Gore's running mate at the time.

Knowing Jorge Mas Canosa's tactic of pitting one party against the other, I was fully in favor of the meeting. Lieberman was a longstanding ally of our cause, and he and Mas Canosa had both been very good friends. Lieberman asked us if he could visit Mas Canosa's tomb. Despite being a registered Republican,

I went with Pepe Hernández, Irma Mas Canosa, and Jorge Mas Santos to meet with Joe Lieberman at the tomb.

The event that was widely publicized and *The New York Times* quoted me as saying, "We are going to support those candidates who support the policies that will bring freedom to Cuba irrespective of whether they are from the Republican, Democratic or Independent parties."

I believed that then, and I believe it today. Regrettably, the defecting directors, diehard Republicans, had forgotten that Jorge Mas Canosa himself had once invited President Clinton to Miami.

I felt guilty about the strife because I was partly responsible for the defection. After the conflict was reported in the Miami Herald, I advised Mas Santos to chastise the dissenting directors. I remember that directors' meeting well. I was angry and seconded Mas Santos's argument that it was unacceptable to complain publicly. Unfortunately, the defecting directors felt insulted and thereafter resigned.

Other developments may have fueled the fire before the resignations started en masse. Jorge Mas Santos helped persuade the National Academy of Recording Arts & Sciences to move its Latin Grammy Awards from Los Angeles to Miami. This irked some of the directors, who thought it undermined the Foundation's policy not to support any events that included Cuban artists.

The defecting directors founded a new organization, but some tried to claim the name "Cuban American National Foundation" for themselves. As the General Counsel for the Foundation, I was tasked with the legal responsibility to fight for the name. I was forced to file suit against someone I considered a friend, Mario Blas Miranda, who had been Mas Canosa's bodyguard for fifteen years.

After Miranda registered a new organization under the

Foundation's name and appointed himself President, I initiated a lengthy and expensive lawsuit to reclaim the name at my firm's personal cost. Somebody else was bankrolling Miranda's legal fight. The judge asked about the source of the funding but never received an answer. Pepe Hernández, Clara del Valle, and others appeared to testify. It was a difficult legal battle because the Foundation's paperwork was in regrettable disarray. The court finally ruled in our favor, finding that our organization was allowed to keep the name because we were using it at the time.

Unfortunately, the defecting directors cultivated a good relationship with George W. Bush and used it to drive a wedge between Bush and the Foundation. George W. Bush gave a speech in Miami that I will never forget. The Bush Administration allowed the leadership of the new organization on the stage while completely ignoring the Foundation. At the very end, after much effort on our part, we were given a few seats in the audience. I remember sitting with Clara del Valle in the bleachers when one of the defecting directors, Feliciano Foyo came up and laughed in our faces. It was a sardonic, angry laugh. The irony was that I was (and still am) a passionate Republican and supporter of George W. Bush.

Shortly before President Obama's election, the Foundation invited the presidential candidates to the traditional May 20 lunch for Cuban Independence Day. We had never had a Democrat as a speaker, as the luncheon had traditionally been limited to the Republican candidates. But then-Senator Obama saw things differently. When Mas Santos advised me that Obama would be the keynote speaker that day, I immediately tried to have Senator McCain come to speak also, but anti-Foundation forces quashed my efforts. I couldn't even get McCain to send us a video.

I was asked to attend the meeting with Obama before the lunch. I declined, explaining that I was working hard for Senator

McCain and felt that my attendance might confuse people. I heard later that when Obama asked what he should say at the luncheon, he was told to support "people-to-people" exchanges and other softer views. My goal has always been to indict Castro for his crimes—a hope shared by many in my community. Obama never mentioned the possibility of an indictment or going after Castro; instead, he just said what he was told to say. When the dust had settled, the Foundation had obtained the largest amount of money ever from a fundraiser.

When Obama spoke, the place was packed. Laly Sampedro called to tell me that donors were offering her up to $5,000 and $10,000 a table. I usually bought two tables at $1,500, but that day I told her to sell them. That day, the Foundation turned from a bastion of Republican ideas into a Democratic beachhead in the Cuban American community. Some said that Jorge Mas Canosa would have turned over in his grave if he had seen it. For me, a positive note was a thunderous speech given at the luncheon by now-Senator Marco Rubio. It is always good to hear Marco speak; he calls it as it is

At a meeting with the directors, I insisted that we could not become a partisan organization. I argued that it would be against all our interests, both legally and logically. My arguments were to no avail. Some in the Cuban exile community even called the Foundation treasonous; the older generation still saw the Democrats as same party that betrayed us at the Bay of Pigs. They had forgotten that Mas Canosa frequently pitted one party against the other to get what he wanted.

During the election season, while working with the Republican Party in Louisiana, I invited many of the directors to come to a fundraiser in New Orleans to raise money for Senator McCain. The event would be held at the D-Day Museum in New Orleans. I had hoped that the fundraiser wouldn't be infested by petty Miami politics—but I was wrong. Once the anti-Foundation forces heard about it, they made a strong effort to ruin the event and ensure that the directors couldn't meet with Senator McCain.

I had arranged for a thirty-minute meeting with Senator McCain. I soon learned that it was reduced to ten minutes. Eventually, I cancelled the meeting and told Mas Santos, Pepe Hernández, and the others who were coming to forget it. The anti-Foundation folks even sent someone to the D-Day Museum to ensure that we couldn't claim to have met with McCain. Believe it or not, the story was actually published as an article in the Miami Herald. Their relentless efforts to humiliate the Foundation and break its bond with the Republican Party continue to this day.

I found it incredibly odd that fellow Republicans would actually interfere with McCain's fundraising efforts. You really have to be a Cuban to understand this mentality. Sometimes I wonder if we don't deserve Castro.

Personally, I only have one enemy, Fidel Castro. I would do anything in my power to bring back the defecting directors. We have a common goal: a free Cuba. Personalities and differences should not keep us divided and weaker. Every Cuban that dreams of a free Cuba is my ally.

Today, the Foundation's quiet but relentless support of the dissidents in Cuba is paying off. The Foundation is united, stronger, and with a clear mission; help the dissidents free Cuba.

THE STRUGGLE HAS ITS
FUNNY MOMENTS: CLARA,
THE DONALD, NEWT, AND ME

CRISTINA AND I ARE VERY GOOD FRIENDS WITH CLARA DEL Valle, Vice Chairwoman of the Foundation, and her husband Mario. Clara and I share a common Cuban trait: we both love to laugh and find humor in the often-ridiculous positions we find ourselves.

Clara is a petite, exuberant woman who naturally becomes the center of attention at every gathering. In her private life, she is a faithful Christian and a Cuban patriot, as befits her heritage as a Bacardi. The Bacardi family—owners of Bacardi, Dewar's, Bombay Gin, and Grey Goose—have been staunch allies in the struggle to free Cuba. Clara is the glue that holds the Foundation together, and she forbids us from arguing with one another. She is truly indispensible—especially since Cubans all tend to have a high opinion of their own opinions.

After "The Donald" (Trump) wrote an op-ed that favored our position on trading with Castro, we invited him to Miami to thank him publicly. Trump was considering a run for President—as usual—so he accepted. When we reached the airport, we saw that a crowd of over two thousand Cuban exiles had gathered, all yelling, "Trump! Trump!" It was clear to Clara and me that this was one of those ridiculous moments in our struggle.

The plane landed, emblazoned with huge letters that read: "TRUMP." Clara had brought two-dozen roses to present to Trump's wife. I sensed she had no idea who Trump's wife was, so I asked her if they were for Ivana. Rather than admit she was unsure, Clara said yes, and we laughed. I soon learned that Trump was hanging with his now-wife, Melania—who I find to be considerably more interesting than her husband.

Jorge Mas Santos and Trump went off in the first limousine; Clara, the flowers, and I went in the second. We had to climb deep inside the limo as a number of young, good-looking women in miniskirts crammed into the vehicle. Knowing it would piss Clara off, I started chatting up the giggling ladies. They each had impressive titles: "Marketing Director," "Advertising Coordinator," and so on. Clara, annoyed because she couldn't hear what they were saying, asked me who they were. I told her we were in the "limo for floozies." She threw the roses at me and demanded to get out, but alas, we were trapped inside.

The rest of the Trump event was fraught with absurdity. We then went to the Bay of Pigs Brigade office, which was packed. All the Cubans had gathered around Trump and were hugging him. Cubans love to hug. Trump asked me to help get them off of him, perhaps fearing for his fine suit and shirt. I told him if he wanted to be president, he needed to get used to Cuban hugs. Mr. Trump didn't seem think I was too funny; however, he was looking for protection, and I was the only Anglo-looking guy in the room. He wouldn't get any help from me. I decided that I was going to have some fun with The Donald.

During a brief moment of silence, a Cuban yelled, "Viva Ronald!" That was good enough for me; henceforth I introduced him to others as "Ronald Trump." He corrected me each time until I told him that, in Miami, his name was Ronald. I just couldn't take this Ronald seriously—his pink yellow hair was up in a bouffant. I was pretty sure he didn't know where Cuba was on the map.

When we arrived at Trump's suite, all the Foundation Directors crowded around him. I opted to chat with Melania, who had a keen wit and was easy to look at. Trump seemed baffled by his new friends; I'm sure he couldn't understand the older Cubans' thick accents. Melania and I joked with each other. She is smart. Once when a reporter came up and asked her whether she married Trump because of his money, she shrewdly countered by asking the reporter whether he thought Trump married her because she was ugly.

Years later, I escorted Newt Gingrich to the Biltmore Hotel for a Foundation event. Cubans were crawling on the walls and yelling in his support. Professor Gingrich seemed terrified—perhaps because the Cubans were mispronouncing his name so that it sounded like they were yelling, "Nut! Nut!" When he nervously asked what they were saying, I gave him a break and clarified it for him. I liked Newt; he really is just a nerdy professor.

At Jorge Mas Canosa's funeral, Clara and I stood guard, military style, next to his casket at the cathedral's altar. We were sad but very proud to be there as thousands passed in front of his casket. To ease our pain, we wisecracked with each other and counted all the pairs of white patent leather shoes. Cubans laugh in sad moments. But our laughter stopped once we saw the hundreds of old and feeble people who stood or sat in their wheelchairs to get one last look at Jorge. Then we cried. You see, Jorge gave us all hope. Nobody else had been able to do that.

Then I saw Clara glaring at the podium, where an arrogant-looking priest was extolling Jorge's virtues. She mumbled to me that but a month before the priest had been extremely critical of Jorge on the radio. No, wait—what she actually said was that she would have liked to choke that son of a bitch. We were all in a highly emotional state, and I cautioned her not to say anything in front of the thousands of onlookers. Secretly, I hoped she would do something, but she was standing too far away from him.

Fortunately, the Good Lord has a sense of humor. There was a changing of the guard, and we filed past the podium towards the ever louder and more loquacious priest. Once Clara had gotten too close, she just couldn't help herself: she let loose a muffled burst of profanities at the priest. Her least offensive insult alluded to his mother and his hypocrisy. The priest stopped his blabbering, turned red, and sat down. My respect for Clara increased exponentially. She made me feel so much better on that sad day.

THE LADIES IN WHITE, LALY "THE ANGEL," AND YOANI SÁNCHEZ

FIDEL CASTRO HAS ENFORCED FIFTY-THREE YEARS OF OPPRESSION over the Cuban people. There are no civil or human rights. Castro has perfected the arts of coercion, intimidation, torture, and murder. Everybody is willing to talk about the embargo, but nobody wants to talk about the horrors of Castro's Cuba. By blaming our government or the Cuban exiles, people can avoid facing the reality of Castro's regime. The whole world has abandoned the Cuban people. Nobody wants to hear about the atrocities because it would make them feel guilty—like they should do something. It's like seeing a starving child on TV and just changing the channel.

Frequently, American tourists travel to Cuba at the behest of the Cuban government and come back with glowing accounts of their trip. That's because they're shown only what Castro wants them to see. Cubans of my generation come back devastated because they know what the country was like before Castro. Cuba now is nothing more than a garbage bin of decaying buildings and poverty. Castro has indeed managed to equalize the classes: everybody there is one step short of starvation. Everyone except for him and his goons, that is. Moreover, the people of Cuba cannot congregate or organize without fear of being reported to the government.

Where is the resistance? Who are the people in Cuba struggling and fighting for what is right? Interestingly, it is the Cuban women who excel in their bravery and courage against the dictator.

In the spring of 2003, Castro's government arrested, tried, and sentenced seventy-five human rights dissidents in kangaroo courts. They were absurdly and arbitrarily accused of terrorism and collaborating with the United States, particularly the United States Interests Section in Havana. Journalists and librarians received prison terms in excess of twenty years.

In response to the arrests, the wives, mothers, sisters, and female relatives of the imprisoned dissidents formed a group called the Ladies in White (*Damas de Blanco*). They all attended the Sunday mass at Saint Rita's Church in Havana to pray for their imprisoned relatives. After mass, they paraded through the streets from the church to a nearby park, wearing white clothing and holding white flowers. They continue this tradition, every Sunday, to this day. Since then the movement has expanded, and the Ladies in White now have chapters in the provinces of Pinar del Rio, Havana, Matanzas, Santa Clara, Holguin, Santiago de Cuba, and Guantánamo.

Castro fears these brave women, but he is too media-savvy to suppress their movement openly. When he wants to break up dissident groups, he sends in agents dressed as civilians instead of uniformed police. Each Sunday, Castro dispatches female agents to "protest" against the Ladies in White during their marches. These "protesters" push, beat, and even arrest the Ladies. Castro wants them to look like normal people willing to defend his dictatorship.

On March 16 and March 17, 2012, seventy members of the Ladies in White were arrested, including Berta Soler, the group's current leader. They had hoped that Pope Benedict XVI would recognize their movement during his trip to Cuba, but his visit was a disappointment. As a Catholic and a man of faith, I can tell you that the Catholic Church has been timid and ineffective against the Castro government. I know that God is with us and with the Ladies in White, but the Catholic Church has been an embarrassment.

Cardinal Jaime Lucas Ortega, the Archbishop of Havana, is a traitor to his faith. On April 24, 2012, he gave a speech at Harvard University where he called a Cuban dissident group—which had occupied a church in Havana and been physically thrown out by security—"delinquents and mentally ill." Ortega has met repeatedly with Raúl Castro. If he is doing anything at all to help the dissident movement, he must be doing it covertly. Jesus Christ openly defied his would-be oppressors. Through his actions and words, Cardinal Ortega has sanctioned the evil work of Fidel and Raúl. Those who pray for Cuba's freedom should look elsewhere, for Ortega is not to be trusted.

I will never forget Pope John Paul II's visit to Cuba in 1998. I was glued to the television, hoping that a miracle would occur with the arrival of this holy man. But Satan has his ways. Once the world's television cameras were focused Cuba and the Pope's historic trip, the Monica Lewinsky scandal broke and took precedence over all issues of actual importance. The world's attention was diverted to that disgusting episode, and the Pope's visit to Cuba was ignored.

The Ladies in White have an angel on earth looking out for them: Laly Sampedro, a good friend of mine and the rest of us at the Foundation. A kind, caring person, Laly keeps in regular contact with the Ladies and works with the Foundation to ensure that these women receive the help they need to continue with their work. Rarely a month goes by that the Foundation doesn't provide them with some form of assistance. Laly ensures that their children are fed, clothed, and housed. She even makes sure that they get presents at Christmas. I never say no to Laly because I know that the help goes directly to the Ladies. I'm happy to give because I truly feel that I am in their debt.

The Ladies in White show no fear. Even though they are spied on and beaten by Castro's thugs, they are always willing to talk to us. When I called Laly to help me gather information for this book, her first question was, "Do you want to talk to the Ladies in White?" Of course I did.

On May 21, 2013, I had the privilege to meet with Berta Soler who was allowed to leave Cuba temporarily. She gave public testimony against Castro and his thugs and plans to return.

A few years back, with the help of Jay Dardenne, the Lieutenant Governor of Louisiana, I obtained a proclamation wherein the people of Louisiana supported the Ladies in White. Laly had them speak to us on the steps of the Louisiana State Capitol via telephone. They did so at their peril—Castro has had people killed for less. I can tell you that they are respectful and grateful women. We've received many letters from them thanking us for the little we do. I feel unworthy of their thanks; after all, they are the ones risking their lives and taking the beatings. I certainly don't need their letters, but they send them anyways.

When you go against Fidel Castro, he strips you of your right to food, electricity, and other basic necessities. He forbids you from working for the government, the country's only employer, and leaves you penniless. Laly speaks with Berta Soler, the group's leader, every day to find out what they need. The Foundation provides them with cell phones and computers. She also sends funds so that the Ladies in White can buy food for their relatives in prison, who would otherwise starve. Berta asked me for clothes and shoes for the children of the dissidents who are in rags.

Once a month, the Ladies in White put on a "Literary Tea" in Havana to share their experiences and write letters to the

Cuban government. Laly gave me one letter that they wrote to Raúl Castro, dated September 17, 2012. It is a very polite letter, which I will now translate:

The members of the movement Ladies in White, as Cuban citizens, demand that you put a stop to the voracity unleashed by the repressive forces against the defenders of human rights and especially against the women of our group.

The Rapid Response Brigades, organized and directed by the government's security forces without any other purpose other than to hunt those who would criticize the government, have attacked and damaged hundreds of activists' houses. To be brief, we will mention two events that occurred within a period of less than a month:

On September 6, 2012, a furious mob, led by the delegate from the communist party, knocked down and destroyed with sledgehammers the home of Lady in White Vivian Peña Hernández and her husband, Misael Valdés Díaz, in the city of Palma Soriano. They broke and stole her personal articles.

In Holguin, on August 18, members of the regular police, the government security forces, and paramilitaries attacked a home where fourteen Ladies in White were holding their literary tea.

During the attack on the home, the mobs beat up, threw rocks, and aimed water hoses against the women; they confiscated books and DVDs; they hit and ripped off the clothes of the young daughter of one of the Ladies in White and terrorized another minor, threatening to imprison him in a juvenile detention center."

Considering that the Ladies in White is a peaceful movement that operates within its constitutional rights,

we ask you that you take energetic measures against the brutality inflicted by the repressive governmental entities at your command and that you stop trying to foment, through your outward statements, hate between Cubans.
—Berta Soler, in the name of the Ladies in White

It was brave of the Ladies in White to write Raúl Castro directly. Now he knows that they accuse him of being responsible.

The Ladies expect the Castro brothers to continue their violence, but they nevertheless display their courage in person every Sunday. On Palm Sunday in 2004, members of the Communist Women's Federation assaulted them. On many occasions, government security police have threatened and harassed them individually in an attempt to put an end to their activities. Berta told me the new practice is to stick them with unknown pointed objects to scare them. Undeterred, the Ladies in White continue to stage their public marches and vigils.

The Ladies in White gain increasing international recognition as their public acts of bravery provoke widespread respect and admiration. In 2005, the Ladies in White were awarded the Sakharov Prize for Freedom of Thought by the European Parliament. The prize recognizes organizations or individuals who have strived for human rights against oppression and tyranny. The Sakharov organization selected five leaders of the movement to attend the award ceremony in Strasbourg, France: Miriam Leyva, Berta Soler, Loyda Valdez, Julia Núñez, and Laura Pollan (deceased), who began the movement and whose husband Hector Maceda is currently serving a twenty-year sentence.

After the Ladies won the Sakharov Prize, Castro forbade any of them from attending the ceremony. Instead, Clara del Valle and Laly Sampedro went to the ceremony as their representatives. The Ladies in White received other prizes from the "Human

Rights First Organization" and the "*Premio Convivencia.*"

While the Ladies in White have received considerable recognition in other countries, the U.S. media largely ignores them. I hardly ever see anything about them in our news.

On occasion, the Ladies have successfully pressured Castro into improving conditions for the prisoners. Berta Soler's jailed husband, Ángel Moya Acosta, suffered terribly from a herniated disc in his back but was given no medical treatment. Mrs. Soler wrote a letter addressed to Fidel Castro at the Communist Party Headquarters and announced that she would stage a vigil at the park adjacent to their offices until her husband was transferred to a hospital. Two days later, in the early morning, government security forces broke up the protest and demanded the women return to their homes. It seemed their cause had lost, but later that day it was reported that Berta's husband had been transferred to Carlos Finley Hospital.

The Ladies in White are not the only women in Cuba working for change. Writer and blogger Yoani Sánchez has achieved international fame and multiple international awards for her brave criticism and realistic portrayal of life in Cuba under the Castro government. In 2008, *Time Magazine* listed her as one of the world's 100 most influential people, stating that, "Under the nose of the regime that has never tolerated dissent, Sánchez has practiced what paper-bound journalists in her country cannot: freedom of speech." President Barack Obama wrote that her blog "provides the world a unique window into the realities of daily life in Cuba." Her blog has been blocked from Internet sites in Cuba, so she has had to rely on Cuban friends to post her texts, which she sends by e-mail.

Yoani has personally experienced the violence of Castro's repression—government agents abducted her in her own neighborhood. On November 6, 2009, Yoani was on her way to an anti-violence demonstration when she was forcefully taken into a car. To intimidate her into silence, the agents beat her severely on her face, body, and knuckles. The assault was so bad that she had to walk with a cane for weeks afterward.

I recently had breakfast with her at the home of Tony Costa in Miami. She was allowed to leave Cuba temporarily. She told me the beatings scared her and showed me a hole in her mouth where they had knocked a tooth out. But her greatest fear is when the security apparatus threaten her only son. She plans to go back to Cuba and continue to blog against Castro. A profile in courage.

THE MURDER OF
OSWALDO PAYÁ

CASTRO RECENTLY KILLED ONE OF CUBA'S BRAVEST DISSIDENTS, Oswaldo Payá. The founder of Cuba's Christian Liberation Movement, Payá was also the creator of The Varela Project. The Project's aim was to collect ten-thousand signatures, which would—under Cuba's constitution—entitle the signatories to a referendum on the dictatorship. Payá collected more signatures than were needed. Not only did Fidel Castro ignore the signatures, he later had Payá killed.

In September 2012, Castro ordered a car to ram Payá and three others off the road. Harold Cepero, another well-known dissident, and Payá were both killed in the crash. Ángel Francisco Carromero, a young Spanish citizen, and Aron Modig, a Swedish politician, were knocked unconscious. When Carromero awoke, he would experience the true nightmare of Castro's Cuba.

I had spoken with Oswaldo from time to time and was deeply impressed. I am free to attack the regime from the safety of the United States, but unlike me, Payá faced the monster in his lair, armed only with his faith and goodness. Hundreds attended his funeral, and many were arrested.

Through lies, torture, and extortion, the Cuban government managed to suppress the truth for months. The Western media repeated the misinformation. Castro's people charged that Carromero had been driving recklessly and crashed the vehicle himself. Video was released of a "press conference" in which a bleary-looking Carromero apparently confessed to accidently crashing the car after hitting a patch of unpaved road.

The trial was held in Bayamo, east of Havana. The prosecution charged Carromero with the equivalent of involuntary manslaughter, seeking a sentence of seven years. In his defense, Ángel claimed that he was going no faster than 50–55 mph. The court found him guilty anyways and sentenced him to four years in jail. Meanwhile, the Payá family decried the trial and asked for an independent investigation. Naturally, their request was denied.

The trial lacked even the pretense of transparency or justice. Payá's family was not even allowed in the courtroom. Yoani Sánchez planned to write a story about the trial but was arrested on the way to the courthouse. She was detained and interrogated for over thirty hours. Freedom House, a human rights NGO, condemned the sentencing and argued that it failed to follow due process of the law. Freedom House consistently places Cuba among the world's most oppressive countries; their survey of political rights and civil liberties ranked Cuba "not free" in 2012.

The Spanish government eventually intervened and negotiated a deal where Carromero would be returned to serve his sentence in Spain. Modig, who claimed to be asleep at the time of the crash, was never charged and quietly returned to Sweden. Although the Payá family continued to demand justice, it appeared that the affair was settled.

When Carromero met Rosa María Payá, Oswaldo Payá's daughter, he knew that he could not stay silent. Her courage inspired him, and although Carromero realized that he would face threats of reprisal and assassination, he decided to tell the truth. On March 5, 2013, Carromero told the whole story in an interview with *The Washington Post*:

> They were following us from the beginning. In fact, as we left Havana, a tweet from someone close to the Cuban government announced our departure: 'Payá is on the road to Varadero.' Oswaldo told me that, unfortunately, this was normal.
>
> But I really became uneasy when we stopped to get gas, because the car following us stopped, waited in full view until we were finished and then continued following. When we passed provincial borders, the shadowing vehicle would change. Eventually it was an old, red Lada.
>
> And then another, newer car appeared and began to harass us, getting very close. Oswaldo and Harold told me it must be from 'la Comunista' because it had a blue license plate, which they said is what the government uses. Every so often I looked at it through the rearview mirror and could see both occupants of the car staring at us aggressively. I was afraid, but Oswaldo told me not to stop if they did not signal or force us to do so. I drove carefully, giving them no reason to stop us. The last time I looked in the mirror, I realized that the car had gotten too close—and suddenly I felt a thunderous impact from behind.

From there, Carromero's story only gets more horrific. He woke up on a stretcher and was soon interrogated by an officer of the Ministry of the Interior. The hospital was full of soldiers who kept him heavily drugged and hooked up to an IV. They continued to harshly interrogate him and started videotaping his every move. He was moved to a disgusting prison that was crawling with insects and rats.

Finally a government representative arrived and gave him the "official" story. Carromero would repeat their lies, or he would be killed. His confession was given under the threat of death and the heavy influence of drugs. Carromero acquiesced to the trial because he knew what would happen if he didn't play along. He remembered the example of Alan Gross, the American who was given a fifteen-year prison sentence for bringing computers to Cuba.

Carromero continues to serve his sentence in Spain. Since his revelation, there have been renewed efforts for an independent investigation into Payá's death. Rosa Maria is lobbying hard for justice for her father, traveling all over the United States and Europe. Even the Obama administration and members of Congress are pressuring the Inter-American Commission on Human Rights to investigate the case. Supporters of the action include senators Bill Nelson (D-FL) Florida, Marco Rubio (R-FL), John McCain (R-AZ), Bob Menendez (D-NJ), Mark Warner (D-VA) and Mark Kirk (R-IL).

This is a fresh opportunity to renew the indictment effort and bring Castro to justice.

THE DISSIDENT GUILLERMO "COCO" FARIÑAS HERNANDEZ

TWENTY-FOUR HUNGER STRIKES IN CUBA'S PRISONS AGAINST the dictator Fidel Castro have left Guillermo Fariñas with the countenance of a victim of concentration camps. Nevertheless, the tall, fifty-one year old, slim man exudes quiet power. He is nicknamed "El Coco" which refers to his bald head. I had the privilege of spending two days with Guillermo who answered all my questions without hesitation or fear. I first met him on May 19, 2013, at a small lunch arranged by Clara Maria del Valle for him and the Ladies in White at the restaurant Havana Harry's in Miami. The next day, I interviewed him for this book at the offices of the Foundation. His small, silent and unpretentious mother sat within a few feet of him at all times, like a guard dog. She is fearful for the life of her son who has repeatedly threatened to give it up for Cuba. Wherever I went with him in Miami, Cuban Americans came to thank him for his courage. They patted him on the back.

Pursuant to a new policy, Castro let him travel to the United States. He immediately denounced the regime as criminals. He doesn't mince words. There is a calmness about him that is perplexing. He told me point blank he was going back to Cuba no matter what and was going to complete his mission, the freedom of Cuba. He had no doubt about that.

Guillermo was born on January 3, 1962, and is a Cuban doctor of psychology, but he is also a journalist and most importantly perhaps now after the death of Oswaldo Payá, the most powerful dissident in Cuba. He was the organizer of *La Unión Patriótica de Cuba*, a dissident group with over 6,000 members, by far the largest dissident organization. He has refused the leadership of the organization insisting that the few that lead it should be all of equal rank. The dissident organization has members throughout the island. Guillermo was emphatic that he was opposed to *"caudillos"* or in English, strong men. He was awarded the Sakharov Prize for Freedom of Thought by the European Parliament in 2012. Castro did not allow him to travel to Strasburg to accept the award. The European Parliament had an empty chair in his place at the ceremony.

Guillermo was pro Castro for many years until he broke with the government. He was a condecorated member of Cuba's Special Forces and fought in Angola. Guillermo respected greatly his superior, General Arnaldo Ochoa Sánchez. Ochoa came from the Camilo Cienfuegos group, the good guys. Ochoa was falsely accused by Castro of participating in illegal drug trade with the Colombian cartel which is precisely what Fidel and Raúl Castro were doing to obtain funds. Castro threatened Ochoa's family if he did not admit to his guilt. Ochoa had evidence that the Castros were participants in the drug trade. Castro knew full well that if Ochoa gave evidence against him on this issue, they could face serious consequences from the United States government so he made Ochoa the scapegoat. Ochoa was by all accounts a brave and charismatic leader who led troops in Angola, Venezuela and Nicaragua. Ochoa was executed and it is said that he insisted on not wearing a blindfold and on giving the order to shoot him. Guillermo believed that Ochoa had effectively been assassinated by the Castro brothers and gave that opinion publicly.

From that moment on, he was a guest of Castro's prisons over and over again.

To make matters worse, once released from one of his imprisonments, Guillermo was working as a child psychologist in a hospital when Fidel Castro came to personally close down a portion of the hospital. Guillermo publicly confronted the dictator and demanded a promise that he reopen the hospital for the children within six months, supposedly after the "special period," which Castro had announced, ended. Fidel became enraged with Guillermo, but made the promise and stormed out of the hospital. Shortly thereafter, Guillermo was elected the leader of the union, but Castro never forgot the slight. Castro never reopened that portion of the hospital.

Thereafter, as union leader, Guillermo engaged in a series of disputes with the female doctor who headed the portion of the hospital which continued to stay open. This doctor was a member of the Central Committee of the Communist Party, the most powerful group in Cuba. She was thoroughly corrupt. Guillermo denounced her corruption publicly. The doctor's family members attacked him physically, but that did not deter Guillermo from continuing to denounce her corruption. The leaders of Castro's Cuba live well because of corruption.

Another major confrontation occurred when Castro brought the remains of El Che Guevara to Santa Clara. Guillermo felt that El Che Guevara was a murderer and did not deserve to be buried in his hometown. He and others began a hunger strike and shortly thereafter he was arrested and condemned to eighteen months which he served in a self-imposed hunger strike.

Guillermo's most famous hunger strikes include one in 2006 when he protested internet censorship in Cuba. Reporters without Borders awarded him a prize. In 2010, he went on another hunger strike to protest the death of his friend, Orlando Zapata Tamayo, a dissident, who died after being ill in Castro's prison and not properly treated. More recently, on July 24, 2012, he was one of many activists arrested during the funeral of the dissident, Oswaldo Payá, murdered by Fidel Castro.

I asked Guillermo what we could do to help him and his dissident organization. He said the dissidents need cell phones and computers to communicate with each other. They also need equipment for audio visual presentations and the publishing of magazines denouncing the regime. Guillermo said that in order to grow, his organization needs financial assistance. Once a person declares himself or herself to be a dissident, the government automatically cuts all assistance and terminates their employment. Therefore, they have no way to sustain themselves or their families. He said that $25 a month was enough for each dissident. He explained to me that ultimately that $25 ends up in the government's hands. Twenty percent is automatically taken away by the government when the money arrives, and the other eighty percent will have to be used in government stores to buy food and necessaries. There are no other stores in Cuba.

Guillermo believes that his dissident movement is growing exponentially and explained that today perhaps if he mounts a demonstration he can put ten to fifteen people protesting the government in front of a police station. However, if he could put 150 people before any police station in Havana, that would change things. He says he is now being approached by Cubans with less fear and that he is encouraged to continue his protests. Guillermo said that he is in contact with high ranking military leaders in Cuba and they are fearful of a sudden collapse of the regime. They are therefore "friendly" with him. They don't want to end up like Qaddafi's people. He says that Castro enjoys little support in the island.

As far as travel to Cuba, he believes that foreign travelers, meaning Americans, Italians, Canadians and Spaniards, do nothing but help the Castro government financially. Like Berta

Soler, Guillermo said that their trips "oxygenate" the government with money. He is, however, in support of Cuban Americans going to Cuba because they then tell the Cubans there how life in the United States is. He also wants Cuban Americans to visit the dissidents that protect and empower them. Guillermo is hopeful and enthusiastic for the future of Cuba. I have no doubt that he will play a leading role in a post Castro Cuba.

CASTRO'S CUBA: A THREAT TO OUR NATIONAL SECURITY

WHILE MOST AMERICANS DO NOT CONSIDER CUBA TO BE A serious threat, our government does. Castro regularly colludes with our enemies, giving them intelligence about the U.S. military and national security activities. From time to time, the FBI arrests Fidel's agents if they become too dangerous. Manuel Cereijo, a friend and a fellow Cuban exile, writes and speaks extensively about these efforts.

Castro has an elite and well-trained military. They are educated at the Baraguá School in Pinar del Río—where the first missiles were discovered during the 1962 Missile Crisis. Colonel Ramírez, a veteran of Angola and Vietnam, presides over the training programs. Castro's soldiers are outfitted with the latest technology, including helmets fitted with head-up displays and thermal, image-intensified, and acoustic sensors. The Cuban military is no paper tiger; it presents a clear and present danger to our country.

Fidel's engineers have extensive experience in electronics, computers, and data processing. They have developed computer viruses to infect U.S. civilian computers. In the recent past, there have been many Cuban cyber attacks on U.S. government computer networks and private corporations.

In 1995, Russia established an espionage base in Bejucal,

south of Havana. The base continues to be fully operational and is outfitted with state-of-the-art equipment. In 1996, Castro started a center for genetic engineering and biotechnology. Cuba has a bilateral biotechnology agreement with Iran; from 1998 to 2001, Cuba built and equipped Iran's major biotechnology center. Evidence of large-scale biological research shows that Castro is producing viable bioweapons.

In short, the notion that Castro's Cuba is not capable of inflicting major damage on the United States is a myth.

Year in and year out, the U.S. Department of State has found Cuba to be a "State Sponsor of Terrorism." Castro is a close ally with all our enemies—including Syria, Iran, North Korea, and Venezuela. Castro's relationships with China and Russia are also well established. He is a friend to anybody who is an enemy of our country.

In *Castro's Secrets*, Brian Latell describes how Castro's intelligence service fielded a world-class operation during the Cold War. Cuban double agents worked right under the nose of the CIA. Latell calls Castro a *"supreme, unchallenged spy master."*

In 1987, Cuban intelligence officer Florentino Aspillaga defected and alerted the CIA to the extent of Castro's spy network. Aspillaga told the CIA that on the day of President Kennedy assassination, he was ordered to stop all CIA tracking efforts and redirect his antennas away from Miami towards Texas. Fidel knew Kennedy was to be killed.

Ana Belen Montes, a Castro spy, infiltrated the highest ranks of our government. She was a senior analyst at the U.S. Defense Intelligence Agency. She had joined the USDIA from the Department of Justice in 1985. She was caught and in 2002 was sentenced to twenty-five years in jail for spying. No repercussions for Fidel Castro from the U.S.

Fidel Castro has controlled Venezuela since Hugo Chavez took power. He now controls Maduro, the new Venezuelan dictator. This will cause great damage to our country, as it has in the past. Aligned with our enemies in Argentina, Bolivia, Nicaragua, Syria, Iran, the Sudan and North Korea, he will continue to foment anti-U.S. sentiment and support terrorist acts against our country. He is only 90 miles away and views himself as the leader of the anti-U.S. world. He is very careful not to get caught but he is always working against our interests and has been successful for five decades.

Once Fidel feels that he is living his last days, he will greatly hurt our country and its people. He should be taken out now, not later.

FINISHED BUSINESS: WHEN CUBA IS FREE

THIS BOOK WILL END ONLY WHEN FIDEL CASTRO IS GONE AND Cubans are free like Americans. Until then this book will be like Andres Oppenheimer's *Castro's Final Hour*[22] or Brian Latell's *After Fidel*:[23] unfinished.

Fidel Castro must be dead, dead, dead; otherwise nothing good can ever happen in Cuba. We must smell his rotten, decaying corpse before we can be sure. Brian Latell, who worked as a CIA analyst, had to listen to all of Fidel's absurdly long speeches (6–8 hours) for his job. Perhaps the most knowledgeable American on Cuban affairs, I think he believes that Raúl is now in command. I must respectfully disagree: I believe Fidel is and has always been in charge.

Raúl Castro is nothing but a comma in Fidel's world; he is impotent and powerless and always has been. If Raúl had enjoyed any true power during his so-called reign, he would have been forced to make dramatic changes in U.S.–Cuba policy. Raúl might be a thug like Fidel, but barring some economic miracle, there is no way he'd be able to control the country in the same way. He lacks the fearsomeness, charisma, and intelligence of Fidel. If he allows any real changes to happen in Cuba, the dictatorship will crumble like a Saltine cracker.

For those who want to know when will Cuba be free and how

we get there, let me analyze the obvious options:

(1) People always talk about the U.S. embargo. Forget it: the embargo is a minor issue in the larger context of Castro and Cuba. The embargo might have stopped Raúl. But for over fifty years it hasn't mattered because Fidel doesn't give a damn whether the people of Cuba live well or not. Most people can't grasp that fundamental idea—he just doesn't care. He only worries about maintaining his power. Children might starve in the streets, but so long as he's in control, he's happy.

Do you think we could have embargoed Hitler out of power? Egocentric dictators are immune to public opinion; they are not threatened by a weak economy, mass unemployment, or anything else that worries politicians in the U.S. The only thing they understand is a gun to the temple. That's why the U.S. had to invade Iraq and pull Saddam out of a hole in the ground with a gun to his head.

(2) It is not realistic to expect that Cubans in the military or the government will assassinate Castro. His bodyguards number over one thousand, nobody is trusted, and even Raúl has to disarm when meeting with Fidel. The ruler is paranoid when it comes to his personal safety. He uses his secret police and Internet espionage to crush potential rebels, and he rewards informants handsomely—or kills them if they know too much.

Soon after his revolution, Fidel created a program called "¿Armas Para Que?" or "Why do we need weapons?" Our American forefathers were wise to protect our right to bear arms, and Charlton Heston knew this as well. Once Fidel stripped the Cuban population of all their weapons, they had no firepower with which to mount a rebellion.

(3) President John F. Kennedy tried to assassinate the Cuban dictator, but Castro's agent in America, Lee Harvey Oswald,

[22] Andres Oppenheimer, Castro's Final Hour, La Hora Final de Castro (Javier Vergara Editor, S.A., 1992).
[23] Brian Latell, After Fidel (Palgrave MacMillan, 2005).

killed him before he could finish the job. Exploding cigars, please. I know many of you are probably uncomfortable with this theory, but as much recent evidence reveals, it's more likely true than not.

(4) Under our present legal framework, it would be virtually impossible for Cuban exiles to successfully make an assassination attempt. As noted earlier, the U.S. government prohibits such acts and carefully monitors Cuban exile activities. The world's leading military power effectively protects Castro from harm.

During the Clinton administration, a group of Cuban exiles was prosecuted in a Puerto Rican federal court for allegedly attempting to assassinate Castro in Venezuela. The U.S. Coast Guard stopped them as they were sailing to the Venezuelan island of Margarita on a yacht carrying heavy firepower. The jury acquitted them after a lengthy trial, but encouraged the defendants to continue their efforts to kill Castro. According to one version of the story, when the U.S. Coast Guard accused one of the purported assassins of drug running, he indignantly replied that they were not drug runners; they were simply going to Venezuela to kill Castro. Apparently the fellow was under the impression that the U.S. government also wanted Castro killed and that he was talking to his allies.

(5) People say that the only solution to Cuba's conundrum is the natural death of Fidel Castro. Upon his death, Raúl will be forced to improve the economy by instituting a hybrid communist/capitalist system similar to China's. This will be his only way to remain in power; however, as Fidel well knows, it will weaken Raúl's control. Raúl has made efforts to reform the country during his years in "power," but Fidel has derailed them all. Once the Cubans starting making money, they will want control of their destiny.

Moreover, Raúl is not as feared as Fidel. If there is a scramble for power between the remaining aged leaders of the revolution, Raúl will likely lose. There is also a semi-organized pro-business group from Cuba's foreign ministry that was recently expelled from leadership. They are quietly waiting to regain power and position.

However, we shouldn't wait for Castro to die. He needs to be brought to justice. We must act now. Here are my ideas:

(1) It's true; Cuba's brave dissidents are not yet fully organized and subjected to horrifically inhuman treatment. Yet, they have the courage to make their voices heard. Guillermo Fariñas is a good example. He is encouraged but they need help. The Foundation supports them and their families in whatever ways we can, but as former Polish President Lech Walesa told me, we must improve their organization and communication.

Recognizing this danger, Castro has blocked efforts to give them access to portable phones and computers. Allan Gross, a U.S. citizen who tried to bring computers to the Cuban Jews, was sentenced to fifteen years in prison for precisely that effort.

Yet we continue to supply them with cell phones and computers. Their ability to communicate has improved greatly. We need to get more such devices into Cuba and help organize the opposition. Yoani Sanchez is a good example of the threat technology presents to the Cuban dinosaurs. Castro is worried; he knows that united they can overthrow him. The Cuban people do not want the Castros and their repressive failed government.

Importantly, the United States and Cuban Americans must get money into the dissidents' hands. Once they declare their dissidence Castro cuts them off entirely, choking their willingness to rebel. They can live off as little as $25 a month. Money is key to the growth of the dissident movement. They don't lack the courage, but they have families to feed.

(2) The world must support these brave dissidents and uniformly reject Castro in every venue. Enough gushing about the monster in Havana. Shout out for freedom in every corner of the world.

(3) Support communications into Cuba such as Radio and T.V. Marti, but ensure that our technology gets the message into every Cuban home. Radio and T.V. Marti are U.S. sponsored productions into Cuba, but Castro blocks much of the transmission. The U.S. obviously has the technology to overcome that; let's do it. Radio and T.V. Marti has a young new and competent leader, Carlos Garcia. He used to be a member of my firm and I know that he is capable and knowledgeable enough to ask for what he needs to fully penetrate Cuba. Let's do it. We need to convince the Cuban people they don't have to accept the dinosaur and tell them what to do to make him extinct.

(4) I am aware of the U .S. Government's "People to People" exchanges where Americans in certain organizations can travel to Cuba. However, I am much more in favor of "People to Dissidents" exchanges. We must encourage visitors to Cuba to visit and support the various dissident movements. Visitors to Cuba should encourage these brave souls and let them know they are not alone. The Foundation can provide names and addresses of the dissidents throughout the island. They want your acknowledgement; it protects them.

(5) Cuban Americans' contributions into Cuba should be limited to only what their relatives absolutely need to survive. Cash remittances to Cuba end up in Castro's pockets.

(6) The U.S. must adopt a policy designed to oust the dictator and free Cuba. For the last 50 years our policy has been to

let Fidel work against our interests worldwide while killing and torturing the Cuban people. The U.S. has acted like Romans joyfully watching Christians being slaughtered in the Coliseum. Americans don't sit idly while human rights abuses are perpetrated. We are the torch of liberty for the world. Let's light it for Cuba. The people of Cuba and the people of America are one. We are next door neighbors.

(7) The Catholic Church needs to act. Cuba is a Christian nation. Our new Pope Francis must go to Cuba and feed the souls of the Cuban people with faith and hope. He must encourage them to demand their freedom. Castro is an atheist who has strangled the church's involvement in Cuba. I am certain the Lord wants better for his people in Cuba but his church must valiantly and openly lead the way. Castro will crumble. He knows what awaits him on judgment day. He was trained by the Jesuits. There is a hell and a place for him there. Clara Maria del Valle and Lady in White, Berta Soler, have just met with Pope Francis and asked for his help.

(8) Cuba is full of Americans spending lavishly in Cuba to Castro's benefit. Our Administration has opened the door without explicitly acknowledging they don't support the travel embargo. They give a wink and a nod to excursion applications they know are not legitimate. Every exempt excursion, like the visit of Beyonce and Jay-Z, results in money going to Castro. Castro's military controls tourism. The door must be shut to everybody but those who will support the Cuban dissidents. Americans should not go there to smoke Cuban cigars and screw twelve year old Cuban girls. Americans are better than that.

(9) Most importantly, the indictment of Fidel Castro for the Brothers to the Rescue murders offers a clear solution. It will automatically weaken him internally and internation-

ally. He will be a target of the U.S. His victims will enjoy a sense of justice. Castro must be held accountable before he dies. He must be indicted in the U.S., the only country he fears. We have the law and facts on our side; we just lack the *cojones* in Washington.

Once indicted, we can arrest him just like we did with Saddan Hussein and President Manuel Noriega of Panama. Then we can declare him what he is, a terrorist, and an enemy combatant. As such, we don't have to read him his Miranda rights, and can interrogate him to find out more about his fellow anti-U.S. terrorists. Following that we can try him in a fair trial and thereafter promptly fry him.

I can't wait to go back. I want to walk the country of my birth, to breathe in the air and let it fill my heart. I imagine seeing the broad smiles of Cuban children enjoying a country that is as free as America. In the meantime, I must content myself with the feelings expressed by my grandmother in her "Epilogue" to *Zafra*:

And now, as I stand by my open window looking down on the street, black and shiny with wintry rain, the thick fog seems to lift its gray veil and I can see across miles and miles of the bluest of waters. On the horizon a long green island is lying in the sun; it is Cuba. A thin thread of smoke curls upward from a tall white chimney; it is Narcisa. The steam is up, the boilers are going; Narcisa is in Zafra. Suddenly I hear the full-throated sound of its big bass whistle; it reaches me distinctly from across the water.

The tall palms of our garden wave their long green feathers as the breeze rustles through them; they seem to call me. Puffing past our old white house, the Rhinoceros

Express toots an impertinent little greeting. Our parrot lets out a demoniacal shriek; a grating sound comes from the kitchen—somebody is grinding coffee. The pungent smell reaches my nostrils; I am breathing it in and it is good. From the patio comes the laughter of happy children and the bark of a playful puppy.

All of a sudden I ask myself, "What are miles, anyway?" That all these things that are hundreds of miles away are so near me; that I can see them, hear them, and touch them. And the answer comes to me. "There is no distance for the things we love; they are never really far away; they are always with us because they are in our hearts."

ACKNOWLEDGEMENTS

Although I am a legal writer, I needed the help of an expert to write this book. I found it in my friend, Ken Atchity. Ken supported me as an editor, publisher and marketer of this book. He and his editor Tom Willkens were able to not only smooth out what was a dry factual account, but actually contributed with their own writing and research. I was fortunate that Ken was producing a movie in New Orleans and therefore I had more access to him. My thanks go to Ken, as well as to Robert Aulicino for designing the cover and interior of this book. To my faithful and patient assistant Rosa Rodriguez, thank you for preparing the manuscript at every stage. Rosa and I have worked together for over 30 years. While supporting my busy law practice she has always been there to assist me in my work for a free Cuba.

AUTHOR'S BIO

GEORGE FOWLER was born in Havana, Cuba, on October 12, 1950. The Fowlers were descendants of the British Consul to Cuba who had arrived there in the early 1800s. Mr. Fowler's grandfather was also named George Fowler. He was a successful sugar planter in Cuba who married a New Orleans native, Lise Perrilliat. Mr. Fowler, his wife, children and grandchildren reside in New Orleans.

On January 1, 1959, Fidel Castro took dictatorial control of Cuba and has ruled with an iron fist for the past five decades. Mr. Fowler became a Cuban refugee in the United States at the age of nine. His father died shortly after their arrival in the United States. Because of the family's dire financial circumstances, he began to work at that age and by the time he became an attorney, he had worked in thirty-six low paying jobs. In 1975, he graduated from Tulane Law School, joined a near 200-year-old law firm and twenty-five years ago opened what is now one of the best maritime, energy, and international law firms in the world. The firm is multi-national with offices in many cities. Mr. Fowler is an active litigator, having come up against some of the top legal names in the country. He has practiced not only in the courts of the United States, but worked on cases worldwide.

Although Mr. Fowler embraced American values and reaped opportunities possible only in America, he never forgot his homeland. Inspired by the bravery of his uncle, Alberto Fowler, who first fought with Castro's forces against Batista, Cuba's dictator, then afterwards against Castro in the ill-fated Bay of Pigs invasion, Mr. Fowler vowed to do whatever he could to oust the dictator and obtain freedom for Cuba. He denounced Castro in every forum he could, starting at the age of eighteen where he met his wife, Cristina, in college.

In 1989, he joined the Cuban American National Foundation, the largest and most powerful anti-Castro organization. He soon was appointed its General Counsel, a position he holds today. Using his legal background, he has tried to have Castro brought to justice for his crimes against humanity. He presented the case before the U.S. Congress seeking the indictment of Castro for the murders of the Brothers to the Rescue pilots, mercilessly shot down by Castro's MiGs within ten miles of the United States. He also sought to have Castro indicted in other countries, including Spain, where he filed a criminal complaint alleging 17,000 political assassinations, torture, imprisonment and rapes by the Castro government. Mr. Fowler has sought to have Fidel Castro arrested and brought to justice. Mr. Fowler has brought legal actions and claims against those who have defamed the Foundation in an effort to weaken its struggle against the Castro government. He assisted as counsel in the Elian Gonzalez case where he denounced Castro's crimes in the world media.

Mr. Fowler has lived in New Orleans for over forty years where he is committed to a variety of worthy causes, including support for the Latin American community, the fight against corruption, civil and human rights, and promoting international trade with Latin America.

Made in the USA
Lexington, KY
23 January 2015